PERCY GOETSCHIUS, *Mus.Doc.*

The Structure of Music

A SERIES OF ARTICLES DEMONSTRATING IN AN ACCURATE, THOUGH
POPULAR, MANNER THE ORIGIN AND EMPLOYMENT OF THE FUNDA-
MENTAL FACTORS OF MUSIC STRUCTURE AND COMPOSITION,
FOR THE STUDENT AND GENERAL MUSIC LOVER

BY

Percy Goetschius, Mus. Doc.

AUTHOR OF

The Material Used in Musical Composition; The Theory and Practise of Tone-
Relations; Exercises in Melody Writing; The Homophonic Forms of
Musical Composition; Elementary Counterpoint; Applied
Counterpoint; The Larger Forms of Musical Com-
position; Masters of the Symphony; etc.

GREENWOOD PRESS, PUBLISHERS
WESTPORT, CONNECTICUT

122983

Originally published in 1934
by Theodore Presser Co., Philadelphia

First Greenwood Reprinting 1970

Library of Congress Catalogue Card Number 72-109736

SBN 8371-4226-1

Printed in the United States of America

To
JAMES FRANCIS COOKE, Mus.Doc., LL.D., L.H.D.
in sincere appreciation

PREFACE

These articles appeared originally in *The Etude Music Magazine,* from September, 1932, to September, 1933, inclusive. They are here reproduced, with a few extensions and corrections, in convenient book form, through the courtesy of Dr. James Francis Cooke, the able editor of *The Etude,* who, in common with the author, believes that their usefulness will thereby be enhanced.

The opening chapter included the following "Introduction," here reproduced as appropriate Preface:

This series of articles is designed for the music lover at large, who will find therein much fascinating and valuable information concerning the factors of musical structure. Therefore I have tried to adopt a simple, intimate diction, not disdaining homely metaphor, and trust thereby to establish a cordial understanding and friendship with my readers.

But I feel that at the core the essays are addressed also to the professional musician and earnest student; for my aim has been (possibly for the first time in music history) to place every item of theoretical knowledge upon an unassailable *scientific* basis; to substitute facts for complacent tradition and theories, often obscure and uncertain; not to correct errors—for there are no actual *errors* in the rules and deductions we have been taught for ages past. The instinct (that intuitive recognition of nature's laws) of bygone generations of theorists was nearly infallible; what they seem to have lacked is that clear, trenchant statement of facts, with their demonstration, which can come only from a positive scientific source, and which alone can make the education of the student rapid, unhindered, free from uncertainty and contradiction.

To prevent misunderstanding, I would confide to the reader that the term "scientific," as employed above, is not to be accepted in its most literal sense; and I believe that the word "accurate" comes nearer to my purpose. The pupil is so often told simply to "do this" or "not to do that," without being supplied with the comforting *reasons* for these instructions and prohibitions. My incentive has always been to furnish the student with these "reasons"—to afford an answer to the intuitive and insistent "Why?"

PERCY GOETSCHIUS.

Manchester, N. H.

PUBLISHER'S NOTE

Dr. Goetschius, during the course of his distinguished career as a teacher of Theory at the Stuttgart Conservatory, The New England Conservatory, and the New York Institute of Musical Art (Juilliard Foundation), has written and edited a long series of musical works of signal importance. While this book is designed for independent use, the reader may desire to refer to some of these other works of Dr. Goetschius:

Applied Counterpoint. (G. Schirmer, Inc.)

Elementary Counterpoint. (G. Schirmer, Inc.)

Essentials in Music History. (In collaboration with Thomas Tapper, Charles Scribner's Sons.)

Exercises in Melody Writing. (G. Schirmer, Inc.)

Lessons in Music Form. (Oliver Ditson Company, Inc.)

Masters of the Symphony. (Oliver Ditson Company, Inc.)

Sixty Chorales by John Sebastian Bach. (Oliver Ditson Company, Inc.)

The Homophonic Forms of Musical Composition. (G. Schirmer, Inc.)

The Larger Forms of Musical Composition. (G. Schirmer, Inc.)

The Material Used in Musical Composition. (G. Schirmer, Inc.)

The Theory and Practice of Tone-Relations. (G. Schirmer, Inc.)

Analytic Symphony Series; for the Piano—Two Hands. (Oliver Ditson Company, Inc.)

BEETHOVEN	Symphony, No. 1, in C major
BEETHOVEN	Symphony, No. 2, in D major
BEETHOVEN	Symphony, No. 3, in E♭ major (*Eroica*)
BEETHOVEN	Symphony, No. 4, in B♭ major
BEETHOVEN	Symphony, No. 5, in C minor
BEETHOVEN	Symphony, No. 6, in F major (*Pastoral*)
BEETHOVEN	Symphony, No. 7, in A major
BEETHOVEN	Symphony, No. 8, in F major
BEETHOVEN	Symphony, No. 9, in D minor (*Choral*) (In preparation)
BRAHMS	Symphony, No. 1, in C minor
BRAHMS	Symphony, No. 2, in D major
BRAHMS	Symphony, No. 3, in F major (In preparation)
BRAHMS	Symphony, No. 4, in E minor
CHAUSSON	Symphony, in B♭ (in preparation)

D'INDY	Symphony, No. 2, in B♭ major
DVORÁK	Symphony, No. 5, in E minor (*New World*)
FRANCK	Symphony, in D minor
HAYDN	Symphony, No. 2, in D major (*London*)
HAYDN	Symphony, No. 6, in G major (*Surprise*)
HAYDN	Symphony, No. 11, in G major (*Military*)
HAYDN	Symphony, No. 16, in G major (*Oxford*) (In preparation)
LISZT	Les Préludes (*Symphonic Poem*) (In preparation)
MENDELSSOHN	Symphony, No. 3, in A minor (*Scotch*)
MENDELSSOHN	Symphony, No. 4, in A major (*Italian*)
MOZART	Symphony, No. 35, in D major
MOZART	Symphony, No. 38, in D (*without Minuet*)
MOZART	Symphony, No. 47, in E♭ major
MOZART	Symphony, No. 48, in G minor
MOZART	Symphony, No. 49, in C major (*Jupiter*)
RIMSKY-KORSAKOFF	Scheherazade (*Symphonic Suite*) (In preparation)
SAINT-SAËNS	Symphony, No. 3, in C minor (*with Organ*)
SCHUBERT	Symphony, No. 5, in B♭ major
SCHUBERT	Symphony, No. 8, in B minor (*Unfinished*)
SCHUBERT	Symphony, No. 10, in C major
SCHUMANN	Symphony, No. 1, in B♭ major
SCHUMANN	Symphony, No. 2, in C major
SCHUMANN	Symphony, No. 3, in F♭ major (In preparation)
SCHUMANN	Symphony, No. 4, in D minor (In preparation)
SIBELIUS	Symphony, No. 1, in E minor
TCHAÏKOVSKY	Symphony, No. 4, in F minor
TCHAÏKOVSKY	Symphony, No. 5, in E minor
TCHAÏKOVSKY	Symphony, No. 6, in B minor (*Pathetic*)
WAGNER	Prelude to *The Mastersingers of Nuremburg*.

Analytic Edition of Mendelssohn's "Songs Without Words" (Oliver Ditson Company, Inc.).

The "Well-tempered Clavichord" of Bach (Oliver Ditson Company, Inc.).

CONTENTS

CHAPTER 1

How We Get the Natural Scale

The majority of students and music lovers of an inquiring mind find no factor of musical material that excites their curiosity and wonder so immediately and persistently as does the scale. Its paramount importance in composition, and the apparently unaccountable irregularity of its formation (I refer to the so-called Natural Scale) afford sufficient excuse for this curiosity and the desire to solve its mystery. And this attitude is not peculiar to present-day students who manifest increasing eagerness to penetrate the secrets of the tone-art, but has existed for centuries.

Should a student approach me with a request that I offer an explanation of the origin of the scale, I must first stipulate that he state, explicitly, *which* scale he means; for a moment's reflection will show that there are a fairly large number of different scales.

Definition of the Term "Scale"

The definition of this musical term is exceedingly simple and accurate: *any* series of tones arranged progressively *in intervals of whole-steps or half-steps* is a scale (tone-ladder). Occasionally one of these intervals is increased to one-and-a-half steps, but the alphabetical order of the notes is not altered. The number of possible combinations of successive whole and half steps is obviously very great, and a multitude of different scales may be, and are, made. (I have read somewhere that Ferruccio Busoni, that meticulous and indefatigable explorer of the undiscovered potentialities of tone-combination, constructed about four hundred different "scales.")

Many Varieties of Scales

Of these many possible scales, there are some half-dozen that are well known and in constant use: there is the major scale (sounded, in C major, on the white keys of the piano); there are the three forms of minor—the harmonic, the descending melodic, and the ascending melodic form of the minor scale; the chromatic scale, in which every progressive interval is the half-step (played

13

on all the keys, white and black) ; also the fortunately rare "whole-tone" or whole-step scale, in which only six letters appear, one being necessarily skipped. Besides these, there are a few abnormal scales, identified with the Turks, Hungarians, Spanish, and so forth, which derive their characteristic, weird effect from the use of the one-and-a-half step intervals, and which are rather of ethnological or historic interest than of technical or theoretical importance. Further, we find some incomplete scales, like the five-tone scale distinctive of Scotch melodies, and the tetrachords (four-tone scales) of the ancient Greeks. And, notably, there are the ecclesiastic "modes" or scales of medieval music, cunningly devised, and so fascinating in their curious contradiction of the principles which govern modern musical usage, that they merit at least brief description here. The ecclesiastic modes or scales were obtained by adhering to the great, intuitively accepted major form (the white keys, for example), but starting at different points; thus, the *Ionian,* corresponding to our major, running from C to C; the *Dorian,* running from D to D (along the white keys), and therefore indirectly related to our D minor, ascending form, but with C♮ instead of C♯—which signifies, "without a leading-tone"; the *Phrygian,* from E to E (a sort of E minor, descending form, with lowered second step—F♮—the "Neapolitan 6th" of modern harmony) ; the *Lydian,* from F to F, like F major with a raised fourth step (an example of which may be seen in Chopin's *Mazurka,* Op. 56, No. 2, measures 53 to 68) ; the *Mixolydian,* from G to G (G major without its leading-tone) ; and the *Aeolian,* from A to A, corresponding exactly to our descending minor form —and often, quite erroneously, cited as the *origin* of our minor.

Ex. 1

And these were not all, for several "plagal" and otherwise modified forms were added to these six chief "modes."

Only One "Natural" Scale

Now, *of all the possible scales, there is only one fundamental or natural scale, namely, our major*—which emerges forthright and inevitably consistent with Nature's law; all the others, by whatever name known, or to whatever technical purposes applied, are simply modified forms of this natural one—modified by the application of the extremely important ornamenting principle of *altered scale-steps,* a process which is so far-reaching and significant in its uses and results, that we must devote a whole chapter to its exposition later.

Therefore, this is the scale, or group of related tones, whose origin we wish to fathom; at any rate, we must begin, obviously, with this one.

Relation of "Scale" to "Key"

Repeated efforts to demonstrate and account for the apparently irregular form of the natural scale, on the part of music theorists during past centuries, have led to no simple conclusive solution; and the reason for this is that they have devoted their efforts to the scale itself, as if that were the primary factor, ignoring the fact that the actual primary original factor is the *key,* and that all melody, including the scale (which is merely one of countless "melodies"), is derived from the key. It is, consequently, necessary first to define the origin of the key—to go farther back than the scale, which is a *result,* and not an independent fundamental unit.

In order to demonstrate the formation of the key, it is unavoidably necessary to make a brief excursion into the realm of mathematics. This is in no sense inconsistent with the essence of music. The law of nature is the law of all life. Pythagoras said, "In the Universe all is *Number* and Order." The aeroplane must start from the *ground;* and the amount of mathematics involved in enabling the plane to soar through the air with the freedom and grace of a bird is truly stupendous. Our mathematical journey shall be made as brief as possible, for music is mathematics only at its base.

The Key as a Family of Tones

The most fitting name I have ever found for the key is a *family of tones.* Nature gathers tones into groups in strict and inevitable accordance with the law of "relation," congeniality, affinity, unity of purpose, in a word, harmony of spirit; for these are the conditions that normally obtain in good, ideal families, in carefully organized clubs, or in any successful and harmonious community. So the very first step in our research must be the clear definition of the relations that exist between tones, and the comparison of the varying degrees of these relations.

Origin of the Key

The sensation of tone is produced, within the ear, by the very rapid vibration or quivering of the air; a speed of about 440 pulses or waves in a second of time transmits the sensation of a^1 (the third string of the violin). The string is firmly tightened, so that the velocity of vibration shall be regular and constant. The number of vibrations therefore determines the pitch, or name, of the tone; hence we say that a tone is represented by a *number,* and, as a natural consequence, the "relation" of one tone to another is defined, prosaically, by the simple comparison of the respective rates of vibratory speed; not, be it well understood, by the comparison of the numbers themselves, but of their *ratio* to one another; for it is rather a question of quality than of quantity. Taking for example the tone c (middle c), the sensory product of about 262 vibrations, and comparing it with one of just double this rate of speed (524), we find that the latter sounds an octave higher. The *ratio* is 1:2, obviously the simplest in nature; the two vibratory motions are fundamentally identical; there can be no conflict of sound-waves, because each stroke of the slower pulse exactly agrees with every other stroke of the quicker pulse; one pulse is thrown in between the pulses of the other. The sensory results are consequently so very similar that a tone and its octave are regarded, in all phases of musical practice, as *identical,* and they take the same letter-name. The "upper" one of the two tones merely sounds clearer or brighter, and is therefore called, by analogy, "higher."

(The terms higher and lower, as applied to tones, are evidently based upon analogy and not upon physical fact. For, as Berlioz says in one of his essays: "the distinctions higher and lower depend solely upon the distance from the center of the earth; a high object is farther from the center than a lower one." Since tones are purely sensations and not physical objects, it is clear that this distinction cannot correctly be applied to them. The keyboard of the piano is, and must be, perfectly level; hence it is anomalous to speak of the right-end tones as "higher," and those of the left end as "lower." The natural analogy, recognized universally, is best accounted for by the fact that the "higher" tone results from a higher rate of vibratory speed; or by the fact that it results from greater *tension,* which is naturally associated with every physical movement upward. Some theorists insist on the terms "acute" and "grave"; but the current names, "high" and "low," are so natural and popular that we shall retain them here, as a matter of course.)

In other words, then, C is C wherever you find it—high or low. Beethoven begins his *Overture* to "Egmont" with the tone F—nothing but F—sounded by every instrument of his orchestra, from the "low" double-bass F, through the F's of the horns, violins, oboes, to the "high" F of the flutes. But it is no more than the one tone, F, in various shades of brightness and somberness. The function of the octave is limited exclusively to such duplication. If you strike the tones C-E-G with the left hand, on the piano, and then strike the same tones C-E-G with the right hand, an octave higher, no structural addition has been made; nothing more than some increase in volume, and an infusion of brighter luster.

This, then, the octave, is the closest tone-relation, the most absolute tone-affinity. It is, so to speak, too good to be of actual *structural* use, since merely adding octaves, above or below, to a tone, conduces to no other result than a kind of erect flagpole, which has little or no architectural significance—height and depth, but no breadth.

The True Basic Interval of Tone Combinations

In order to gain architectural results, the plan must be widened out, so as to embrace other degrees of tone-relation, which, though still cohesive and unified, will disclose sufficient *differentiation* to constitute distinguishable material for the building of an actual expanded tone-structure.

So we turn to the *next* of the simple ratios, 1:3 (or 2:3, which is practically identical, as shown previously). Two strings vibrating in this ratio produce the so-called *perfect fifth;* for example, C (262) and G (393). It can be located on the piano keyboard by counting upward seven half-steps.

Ex. 2

This *new interval is therefore the true beginning and all-embracing basis of the entire elaborate complex of tone-association.* It is a perfectly harmonious union, the closest relation beyond the unison or octave, and still sufficiently different in its pitch-effect to assure the quality of an independent factor, admitting of combination into new harmonic forms. So close is the relation that one cannot hear the one (C) without thinking of the other (G), and, in the great majority of chords, where the one is present the other will be found in its company; the perfect fifth thus naturally and inevitably pervades all normal music.

Evolution of the Key

The very first use to which this basic interval is put, in musical development, is the formation of the key—the tone-community within which all the evolutions of tone-association are to be consummated. The head of the family (keynote, or tonic) may be any tone—anyone may organize a club. Adopting C as the keynote, it follows, from the above demonstration, that this tone will elect G (his perfect 5th) first of all, as next member. G will in like manner draw in his tone-affinity (perfect fifth), D. D will bring A into the "family," and A proposes, and elects, E. These five (C, G, D, A, E) form the inner circle (or as I have called it, the *nucleus*) of the key of C. They are, as it were, the charter members. They are the tones of the 5-tone "Scotch" scale, and in none of their combinations is there any interval smaller than the whole step, which, though appreciably dissonant, is not disagreeable enough to provoke undesirable conflict. (The whole-steps appear between C and D, D and E, G and A).

But to these five are added two other (extra) tones, one at the bottom (F, a perfect 5th *below* C) and one at the top (B, a perfect fifth beyond E), in a wider circle, which brings the number of members up to seven, *in order to fill out the octave scale.* Thus:

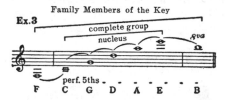

Family Members of the Key

Ex.3

complete group

nucleus

perf. 5ths

F   C   G   D   A   E   B

Note that the two extra tones, F and B, introduce the *half-step* into the community (between F and E, and C and B), which is so much more stridently dissonant that it automatically inhibits the addition of any other extra tones to these seven; for example, a perfect fifth beyond the highest B would be F♯—a tone so boldly antagonistic to the low F that the two cannot be tolerated together in the same community; and if this leaves the question open, "Why not discard the F instead of the F♯?" the answer is that F is so intimately related to the keynote itself, that its place in the key is absolutely assured. Note also, that the keynote is not the *lowermost* tone in the whole group (as might be deemed imperative) but the *second tone from the bottom*. The reasons for this are clearly indicated in the foregoing demonstration: it is the *lowermost tone of the nucleus*.

These five nucleus tones are often used in melodies, without the two "extra" tones. Examine that characteristic Scotch tune *Auld Lang Syne* (Ex. 53.); it contains only the nucleus tones. Also the theme of Weber's *Turandot* Overture; also the chief theme of Beethoven's Overture, No. 3, to *Leonore;* and, most striking of all, the *entire* right hand part of Chopin's Etude in G flat, Op. 10, No. 5 ("black-key" study). And that reminds us that the black keys are the *five nucleus tones* of G♭ (or F♯) major.

The Scale Identical With the Key

These seven tones, then, constitute the key (or family, or club) of C; *and they are the seven tones of the natural scale.* Simply place them closer together, by using the octave-relation, in a row of progressive pitches (whole-step and half-step intervals) and the scale stands revealed. Thus:

This answers every question which has puzzled students for ages: "Why are there just seven tones in the Scale?" "Why are they arranged irregularly in distances of whole- and half-steps?" "Why are the half-steps between tones 3-4, 7-8?" The one sweeping answer, almost silly in its simplicity, is: "Because it *is* so; because, when you place the seven tones of the key in a close row, *it comes out that way,* and could come out in no other way."

So, this, then, is the scale as defined by natural law—the natural scale. And since it is in accurate accord with the workings of nature's immutable law, we need not wonder that the *instinct* of our forerunners recognized this relation, and soon adopted this association of tones in a scale, even long before they had a clear conception of the reasons for it. They *instinctively* perceived the validity of both the octave and the perfect fifth.

Another method of making this clear to the student is worth suggesting. Should the student ask you, "Why is there an A in C major?", you reply, "Because there is a D there." For D-A is the perfect fifth, the basic interval of tone-affinity, the Damon and Pythias of music. Where the one is, the other is very likely to be. If the student pursues his query, "But why is there a D there?" you answer, "Because there is a G in C major," and so on. Or, negatively, if he asks, "Why is there no A♭ in C major?" you answer "Because there is no D♭ there."

There is still another illustration of the formation of a key, which I cannot neglect to add, namely: the entire sphere of innumerable tones represent an infinite chain, each link of which is a perfect fifth from its neighbors. Thus (to note only a small segment of the chain):

Ex. 5.

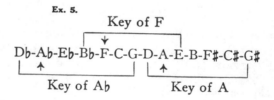

The key consists of any seven contiguous links of the great chain, the lowermost but one of which is the keynote. The student may verify this, from the foregoing example, in which the keys of A♭, F, and A are marked off.

It may be necessary, to forestall criticism, to admit that in the inexorable scientific location of these pitches there are slight discrepancies. For instance, the whole-step from C to D is a trifle (the so-called comma) larger than that between D and E. But this and other discrepancies are so slight as to be negligible; and, with our universal equalized temperament (tuning), they disappear entirely, anyway. Furthermore, where in violin playing, and in singing, the discrepancy may be present, the harmonic instinct of the performer "accommodates" itself, and removes any undesirable consequences.

Finally, no reference has been made to the much-exploited "overtones," because it is wholly superfluous to do so. The only practical function of the overtones is to qualify the *timbre* (tone-color) of various tone-producing, media; wherever they seem to dictate (and surely do confirm) the aggregation of the tone scale, they merely prove the unity of nature, the intermeshing of all the manifold units of the intricate musical apparatus.

SELF-TEST QUESTIONS

1. What is the definition of the term "Scale"?
2. Name the half-dozen Scales in constant use.
3. Name the six medieval Modes, and explain the manner in which they were formed.
4. What must we first define, in order to explain the Natural Scale?
5. What suggestive name may we give to the "Key"?
6. Explain the origin of the Octave, and of the Perfect Fifth.
7. Which is the true basic Interval of all tone-combination, and how is it applied in the formation of the "Key"?
8. Name the Nucleus-tones of C major, and explain the addition of two extra tones to these.
9. How does the "Scale" emerge from the Key?
10. Why is there a B in C major? And why is there no B♭ there?

CHAPTER 2

The Story of the Intervals

There is probably no such thing in the universe as absolute isolation. Every animate being, at least, seeks companionship. And so it is, also, with tones. A single tone, no matter how often repeated nor how far prolonged, can be of but extremely limited use in the structural processes of music. The briefly isolated, ominous horn tone, with which Wagner begins the *Overture* to his opera "Rienzi," is, in point of scientific fact, not totally isolated, for it is accompanied by its "overtones," although these merely define its tone-color as horn; and other tones soon join it, anyway. It is only by adding tone to tone that musical results can be obtained.

When any two tones are sounded together, the effect produced is a dual sensation which musicians call an *Interval*.

This term, like the words "high" and "low," is applied to tones by analogy only. For, since the word "interval" refers to distance or space, it is evident that it is anomalous to apply it to tones, because the latter are not physical entities in space, but incorporeal, intangible sensuous or mental impressions which cannot be located in terms of distance, any more than the word, "interval," can be applied to family relationships. We cannot say that an uncle is so and so many "feet" farther removed than a father. It is true, however, that there are measurable "intervals" between the keys and stops on musical instruments, and also between the *notes* on a music sheet, and this accounts for the adoption of the term. It would seem more accurate to speak of the "relation" of a fifth, an octave, and so forth, instead of "interval"; but the current word is so thoroughly ingrained in musical phraseology that it would be dangerous to substitute any other one for it.

Definition of Intervals

An interval, then, is the association of any two tones, either exactly together, or in succession. The following intervals

Ex. 6

Scale line of C Major.

correspond to the small words and syllables of our language. And just as the child embarks upon his educational career by learning his *a-b, ab,* so the very first thing that engages the attention of the music student is the formation of the intervals; for these are the primitive "words" that make up the musical phrase, and they are the first clues to the *meaning* of the phrase.

Intervals are (or should be) always counted *upward* (the lower of the two tones being one, or prime) *and always along the line of the major scale of which the lower tone is the keynote.* Only by maintaining this rule can the name of the interval be quickly and infallibly determined. And the interval-names are clicked off like the inch marks on a yardstick—*along the scale.*

Thus, the union of C and D is a second, because D is the second step in the scale of C; C and E form a third; C and F a fourth—and so on. The reason for insisting upon the scale-line is, that intervals of the same numerical name may differ in *quality* (for instance, there are four different kinds or shades of the seventh)—and there must be a fixed standard by which these distinctions can be clearly defined.

As we join the other, higher, tones of the scale to its keynote, we obtain, for the *second, third, sixth* and *seventh,* that variety of interval which is known as *major;* while the *fourth, fifth* and *octave* (and also the *unison*) are known as *perfect* (see Ex. 6).

It is obviously not necessary to go beyond the octave, because the list, from there on, is simply repeated; still, there are occasions when the terms ninth and tenth (sometimes even twelfth and fifteenth) are used for some special technical distinction. This is not necessary, and it is rarely done; for C-D is a second, no matter how far above C the D may chance to lie.

In E major, to give an additional illustration, the scheme is this:

Ex. 7

Scale of E Major.

Why are these intervals of the major scale (the "natural" or "standard" intervals) thus diversified? Why are four of them perfect and the other four major?

There are, of course, perceptible aesthetic and emotional qualities inherent in the separate intervals, but of these we must speak later on; the above questions concern at present only the technical conditions.

As to the *perfect* intervals, the answer is simple: recalling that the term "interval" signifies *relation,* it is evident that the perfect intervals are so qualified because they are *perfect relations.* It was amply disclosed, in our preceding chapter, that the fifth and octave constitute the fullest degree of intimacy and affinity that can exist between one tone and another; their tone-relation is perfect. As concerns the interval of the fourth, that is equally perfect, because it is simply the *inversion* of the fifth.

Inversion of Intervals

The inversion of an interval is obtained by reversing the letters, so that the lower tone becomes the upper: the inversion of C-G is G-C; the lower tone is shifted an octave, and, since "a tone and its octave are practically identical," the inversion is merely another shape or aspect of the selfsame harmonic unit. Therefore, since the fifth, when inverted, becomes a fourth, it follows, as stated above, that the fourth also is a perfect interval. The unison, being the inversion of the octave, is, like the latter, also perfect.

In explaining why the other four scale tones are distinguished as *major,* one has not quite so easy sailing. But patience and reasonable concentration will make this clear.

First recall your Latin and realize that the word "major" does not mean "great", but "the greater"; it is not a positive, but a comparative adjective. It is therefore not absolute, but is dependent upon some other quantity or quality with which it is compared. A "greater" (than what?) involves a "smaller" as its counterpart. This smaller dimension is of course the *minor.* From which we conclude that major and minor are two aspects of the same object; *each major interval has its reciprocal minor form,* and their exchange, also, is due to inversion.

It appears, then, that while the perfect intervals are single, complete, independent relationships, the other ones have a dual quality—are either "greater" or "smaller" according to their position, or the point of view of the observer. The perfect intervals are properly so called, inasmuch as their inherent quality is not subject to change; the others are *imperfect,* precisely because they do not possess this inherent stability. One may visualize a perfect interval as a sphere (hence "perfect") which presents always the appearance of the same round body, from every point of view; whereas the imperfect interval is comparable to an oval, or egg-shaped, body (hence "imperfect"), one end of which is smaller and the other larger, thus assuming contradictory forms, as viewed from one side or the other. In homely words, major and minor are the two different ends of the same egg—the difference becoming recognizable only by turning the oval around (that is, by inversion).

Minor Intervals

A minor interval is the result of contracting the corresponding major one; and this is effected by means of an accidental which chromatically lowers the upper tone one half step—the *letter* remaining the same. Thus: the major sixth, E-C♯ (see Ex. 7) becomes a minor sixth by lowering the C♯ to C♮. And the same proceeding holds good for every major (scale) interval. For example: "A", Scale of E major, "B", scale of C major.

Ex. 8. A Scale of E Major.

Maj. Min. Maj. Min. Maj. Min. Maj. Min.
  2nds   3rds   6ths   7ths

B Scale of C Major.

Maj. Min. Maj. Min.
  3rds   6ths

Reverting to the function of inversion, as responsible for the exchange of major and minor, take, for instance, the interval C-E. This is a *major* third. Its inversion, E-C, is a *minor* sixth (as seen in Ex. 8). So we see both terms applied to the *same notes*—not the same *interval,* be it well understood, but to the interval on the one hand, and to its *inversion* on the other. Therefore, since an interval and its inversion (by virtue of the octave-relation) are practically identical, and are built with the *same notes,* it follows that major and its reciprocal minor are simply two different aspects of the selfsame tone-unit.

What I wish to make clear is, first, that an interval and its inversion are essentially the same musical factor. C-E and E-C are the same tone-union, whether C is at the bottom or at the top; inversion does not change it, any more than a rod turned upside down becomes anything else than a rod. The *name* of the interval differs: C-E is a third, while E-C is a sixth; but the harmonic partnership is not altered or affected. There will be certain modifications during the technical performances of the two intervals, just as a person will assume a different decorum in his office from what he affects on the golf course or at a dance—without in the least changing his *personal* identity or nature.

And the second point to be emphasized is that, in these two different forms (original and inverted), we find both the major and minor qualities present at opposite ends, so to speak, as inherent counterparts.

Summarized: a perfect interval when inverted is again perfect; a major interval when inverted becomes minor; and a minor one, likewise, becomes major by inversion.

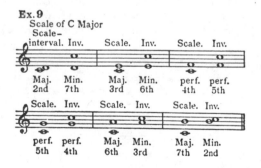

It must be borne in mind that the *major* dimension is the one that always conforms to the *scale-line* (Exs. 6 and 7); and that is the reason why the natural form is called the *major* scale.

Further, the major second corresponds everywhere to the *whole steps,* and the minor second to the *half steps,* in the natural scale.

An illustration of the use of various standard intervals in the progressive structure of a musical sentence may prove interesting and enlightening to the reader. The following occurs in the Symphony in G Minor of Mozart (key of G):

Ex. 10.

Min. Maj. Min. Min. Min. (perf. 5th)   Min. Maj. Min. Maj.
6th 3rd 3rd 3rd 3rd   3rd 3rd 3rd 3rd

And the reader may, if so inclined, define the following chain of
intervals, from Mendelssohn's Op. 16 (key of A):

Ex. 11.

These three classes of intervals, the perfect and "imperfect"
(major and minor), or *standard* intervals, are the staple and
etymological storehouse of musical composition; by far the most
frequent and intelligible tone-unions.   Nine-tenths of all music
are (or should be) made up of these intervals.

Augmented and Diminished Intervals

But there are two other classes, the diminished and the augmented intervals, which, because of their striking characteristics,
serve the purpose of contrast, vitality and urge, and are therefore
extremely important and indispensable, when used in reasonable
proportion to the standard ones, and in their proper places.

Augmented intervals are derived from the *perfect* and the
major, which latter may be enlarged by raising the upper letter
a chromatic half-step (by means of an accidental), *the letter-
names remaining unchanged.* Thus: C-G, the perfect 5th, becomes
an augmented 5th when G is raised to G♯.   And the same with
all *major* intervals also.   (See Ex. 13.)

Diminished intervals are a little confusing because they do not
proceed thus directly from all of the *scale* intervals—perfect and
major (Ex. 6)—but are obtained from perfect and *minor* ones,
by similarly lowering the upper letter.   Thus, the perfect 5th,
C-G, becomes a diminished 5th when G is lowered to G♭; and
the *minor* 7th (for instance), E-D (Ex. 8), becomes a diminished
7th by lowering D to D♭.

Lowering the major interval, it must be remembered, results
in the *minor* form; and it is this latter, the minor, that must be
contracted in order to secure its diminished form.   In other words,
the perfect intervals become augmented or diminished at once
by raising or lowering the upper letter; whereas the major ones
must be lowered *twice* in order to become diminished.   The results
can always be verified by the rule that all augmented intervals

when inverted become diminished; and, *vice versa,* the inversion of a diminished interval gives the augmented form.

Augmented and diminished intervals are comparatively rare —in some cases chimerical; one feels disposed to call them "distorted" intervals. But they have their legitimate uses in composition; and they are now and then still further "distorted" into double-augmented or double-diminished forms. Thus, one of the C major chords (say D-F-A-C) may contain the union of A♭ and D♯ (as "altered" steps), which is a double-augmented 4th; its inversion, D♯-A♭, is a double-diminished 5th.

Ex. 12
C Major

Chord   doub. augm. 4th   doub. dim. 5th

Some of these "distorted" intervals are, as stated, chimerical; that is, they exist only on paper, as logically correct but impracticable deductions—for instance, the diminished 2nd, or augmented 7th.

Enharmonic Distinctions

Great caution must be exercised, in computing intervals, not to alter the letter-names of the tones involved or to confound the accidentals—for example, not to call g♯ an a♭, as, say, in the interval C-G♯, which is an augmented 5th, while C-A♭ is a minor 6th. Such tones (called enharmonic equivalents) are, it is true, produced by the same key of the piano-keyboard, because of the equalized temperament used in tuning. But in point of fact, enharmonic tones, such as g♯ and a♭, though very close in pitch, represent an extremely remote degree of tone-relationship; they lie very far apart in the great chain of perfect-5th links (twelve degrees, to be explicit), and therefore there should be no reasonable doubt as to which one of the two is intended and required.

A few examples of the permutation of intervals should suffice here. Thus, from the tone G, scale of G major:

Ex. 13.

Thirds   ?   Fourths

Maj.   Min.   Aug.   Dim.   perf.   Aug.   Dim.

Fifths   Sevenths   ?

perf.   Aug.   Dim.   Maj.   Min.   Aug.   Dim.

The reader may cypher out the whole list for himself, if so minded; or better, he may try his hand at naming some of the intervals he encounters in the music he is playing, something after the manner indicated in this illustration, in which all the more common intervals are present:

Ex. 14

Min.perf.Maj.Maj.Min.Aug.Maj.Aug.   Dim. Maj. Dim.perf. Aug.
3rd 8th 6th 3rd 3rd 5th 3rd 4th   5th 3rd 7th 5th 6th

perf. Maj. perf. Min. Dim. Min. Min.   perf. Min.perf.Maj.perf.
8th 2nd 4th 7th 5th 3rd 6th   5th 7th 4th 3rd 8th

The foregoing example lays no claims to being a musical conception, for it is a preponderantly mechanical product—a list of diversified intervals. At the same time, it should help to confirm the fact that the labor of composition is more than a stringing together of intervals, with little or no evidence of discrimination. There is the higher law, to which the choice of tones is subject. To be sure, the separate intervals possess sufficiently distinctive emotional qualities and emanate from well defined harmonic sources; and for that reason they can and do exercise functions, partly pre-defined, partly arbitrary, partly urgent, which invest them with a vitality of their own which in turn infuses itself into the life of the musical discourse.

Emotional Attributes of Intervals

Music critics have indulged in much speculation, usually sane but in some cases extravagant and visionary, as to the emotional attributes of the various intervals. The existence of such attributes cannot be gainsaid, and they are in most cases so plainly evident, so universally recognized, and so happily in agreement with the very names themselves, that they must be regarded as definite enough to form an important part of the vocabulary of musical speech.

Thus, the *perfect* intervals possess a pure, clear, open, quiet character; the *major* ones, as the adjective suggests, are manly, strong, convincing; the *minor* ones, obtained by depressing the stature of the interval (lowering the upper tone), have a corresponding depressed, timid, melancholy quality that distinguishes minor compositions from major ones, even to the uncritical hearer, and makes them appropriate for sentences of a somber, pathetic, sad character; the *augmented* intervals betray their stretched, strained quality, which lends stress and urgent action to the current of musical thought; and, finally, the *diminished* ones are of a far more pronounced melancholy, sorrow-laden quality, and always introduce dramatic, almost tragic, hues into the musical portraiture. A very striking example of the use of the diminished 7th may be studied in the profoundly pathetic *Adagio* of Beethoven's piano *Sonata, Op. 106* (measures 5 to 13, 29, 30, 32, 33, and so forth). As a rule, the great classic masters make very discreet use of these subjective attributes, being guided rather by the fundamental requirements of tone-association than by the poetic and romantic or dramatic suggestions which the intervals invite; and the disposition to utilize these attributes as actual parts of speech, or as quickening flashes which illuminate the musical pattern, is one of the very things that signalize the infusion of the *Romantic* spirit into the music of the post-classic era (Berlioz, Schumann, Wagner and so forth). A demonstration of what Wagner (to mention only one of the Romantic masters) has done with the iridescent shades of the interval family (quite aside from their purely technical characteristics) would fill volumes.

Inherent Tendency of Intervals

It remains to add a few significant words respecting the *inherent tendencies* (or the "direction") of some of the intervals.

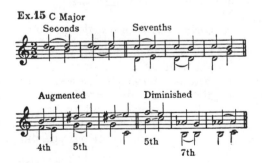

All standard seconds pull apart, or outward. The tones repel each other. Thus: C-D (struck together) will, under normal conditions, pass into B-D, or into C-E, or into some other larger interval.   Their inversion, the sevenths, pull inward—the tones attract each other.   All perfect intervals, and the standard thirds and sixths (i.e. the major and minor ones), are passive—they possess no pronounced inclination.   All augmented intervals are decidedly active, and, normally, draw apart; their inversion, the diminished ones, draw inward.

SELF-TEST QUESTIONS

1. Why is it inconsistent to speak of "high" and "low" tones?
2. Define the term Interval.
3. How are Intervals always counted?
4. What specific names are given to Intervals which agree with the Natural scale?   Four are ——?   and four are ——?
5. Define Inversion, and demonstrate the origin of the term "minor."
6. What is the Inversion of the Major 7th?   Perfect 5th?   Major 3rd?
7. How are all Augmented Intervals formed?
8. How are the Diminished Intervals formed?
9. Define the Enharmonic distinction.
10. What are the inherent tendencies of the various intervals?

CHAPTER 3

How We Get the Chords, and How They Intermingle

The source and genesis of all music are the chords; without some knowledge of them one can obtain no intelligent impression of any music. Therefore it is of the utmost moment to the music lover to acquire at least a speaking acquaintance with them.

First of all, the term, "chord," as used in English musical terminology, is a curious misnomer. For the word "chord," in its original and figurative sense, signifies a single string; and yet it is applied in our language to a cluster of three or more different tones. The word employed for this purpose in the principal European tongues is *Accord* (German, *Akkord;* French, *Accord;* Italian, *Accordo*) and this is the correct word, since it indicates the very condition upon which the formation of a chord is based; namely, a cluster of tones which *accord* with one another, in harmonious union. Our English word is an abbreviation or corruption of the proper term, by a careless omission of the first syllable. Nevertheless, it is impracticable, and would be unwise to insist upon the re-establishing of the original form, and we must therefore persist in calling this musical unit a "chord."

Definition of Chord

A chord, then, is a combination (either together or in succession) of three, four or five tones, so chosen that the resulting intervals are wholly, or at least preponderantly, consonant or harmonious. The chord is therefore the body of tones next larger than the simple interval. There are cases, it is true, in which two tones, properly placed, may suffice to define a complete chord: thus, the two tones, C and E, may clearly indicate the full chord of C major, since such omissions of certain parts of chords are not only possible, without endangering their identity, but in many circumstances frequent and even obligatory. (See chords 5 and 6 in Ex. 18).

However, the genuine chord is assumed to contain no less than three tones, and the full definition of the word is thus stated: a chord is the union of three, four or five tones (*never* more than

five), placed *one above another in intervals of contiguous thirds.*
The chord of C, for example, will surely contain C, and equally
certainly it will contain the tone G, for this latter is the perfect
5th of C, and therefore its most closely related companion-tone
(as demonstrated in our first chapter). To these two is added
the tone E, which is a harmonious, accordant interval with each
of the others. The cluster C-E-G is thus seen to conform to the
definition of a chord. Glance at Ex. 17.

The most important of these three tones is, naturally, the C;
for the whole column is built upon, or rather emerges out of,
that tone; for this reason it is called the *root* of the chord, and
supplies the *name* of the chord—in this instance "the chord of
C." The other two tones are called the third and fifth of the chord
(chord-3rd and chord-5th) according to their interval-distance
from the root.

The Triads

A chord of this kind, consisting of three tones (root, third
and fifth) is known in musical phraseology as a *triad;* and the
formation, the location and the relative values of the triads in a
key are the foremost matters to be thoroughly understood. In
order to make this clear, it is necessary to revert to our demonstration of the key and scale (in the first chapter), and to repro-
duce here the table there given of the key, or tone-family, of C:

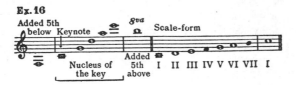

Ex. 16

Triads can be, and are, erected upon every tone of the key,
or scale—*but only the five nucleus tones can be actual roots.* The
triads built upon the two extreme "added" tones (above and
below) are derived from two of the genuine ones and pertain to
the group of so-called incomplete chords—"incomplete" because of
the omission of their root (an apparently startling procedure, but
one which is not at all uncommon and which we shall investigate
and explain later on).

The chords take their names from the scale-step upon which
their root stands; and, for convenience, they also take a number-
name, in the same connection. Thus: the chord upon (or of) the

keynote, in Ex. 17, is the chord of C, or the *One* (step number I in the scale), also called the *tonic* chord. The next one above it is the chord of G, or the *Five*—or the dominant chord; the next one is the chord of D, or the *Two*—or, the second-dominant chord (a name I have proposed instead of supertonic because it is the "dominant of the dominant," or the second perfect 5th from the tonic); then the *Six,* and finally the *Three.* The added chord below the keynote is the subdominant chord, or the *Four;* the added chord above the rest we shall call the *Seven,* although there is a more correct name for it, which will be presently shown. Thus, in the key of C:

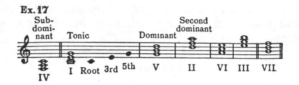

This brings us to the significant problem of the *relative importance* of these chords within a key; for thereby are determined all of their activities (normal or otherwise), their comparative frequency, their customary location, their validity in establishing their key, and all the conditions which prompt the composer in his choice. The degree to which he realizes and respects these distinctions will be largely responsible for the saneness and purity of his music—at least in all of its *technical* aspects.

The most weighty of all chords is that upon the tonic, or keynote (the One). It is usually the first chord in a composition, and is (or should be) the last one; for the essence of the I is *repose,* stability, centrality; it is the Zeus of the musical hierarchy; its disposition is passive—it will not move unless pushed—but it attracts all the other chords to itself, suggestive of the operation of the law of gravity toward the center or point of rest (glance at Ex. 23).

Now, the relative importance of each one of the other chords *depends upon its distance from the tonic,* in the chain of perfect fifths. I always envisage the chords as a row of, say, telegraph poles, which, to the observer standing beside the I, appear to grow smaller and smaller in perspective, until the last one (VII) is so indistinct as to arouse doubt of its being a "pole" (genuine chord); the lower added chord (the IV) is seen, also somewhat indistinctly, over the shoulder. This is exactly the way that nature plants the chords; and well for the composer if he grasps and heeds that arrangement.

According to this theorem, the second in importance is the dominant chord (the V, Ex. 17); it is extremely active, as lively and urgent as the I is passive, and for that very reason in some respects even more useful than the I, especially as concerns its vitality and the force and insistence of its movements.

Next in rank are—not one, but *two* chords together: the second-dominant (the II) on one side, and the sub-dominant (the IV) on the other; *for these two apparently separate chords* (II and IV) *are actually identical* in character, purpose and movements. The exposition of this will be taken up presently.

These second-dominant chords are extremely useful in music, as the chief element of contrast with the more prevalent tonic and dominant chords.

Next in rank follows the Six, which is much weaker, less frequent, and less indicative of its key than the II, and seems to derive its importance mainly from its resemblance to the tonic chord—of which it is usually considered a satellite and for which it is occasionally substituted. (In other words, the VI is regarded in harmony as the *parallel* of the I and is therefore classed as an inferior member of the tonic family.)

The "Baby" Chord

Finally there is the Three, the "baby" of the chord-family, most distant from, and consequently least related to, the tonic. (The III resembles the V, and is regarded as a parallel, or member, of the dominant family.)

As to the so-called Seven (Ex. 17), it claims and maintains a far more significant place than its apparent location "away up in the air" would seem to indicate. It is really a dominant chord. The explanation of this, too, will shortly be given.

Setting aside these last, more remote, chords, as of inferior consequence, we return to the tonic and his near relatives, and realize that they are the actual basis of the entire tone-edifice. The three classes which head the list (the I, the V, and the II + IV) are the tripod upon which all musical structure securely rests. Hence, the I, V, and IV are known as the *principal* triads; in the major key they are called major triads, since their third has the major form; the others (II, VI and III) are minor triads, with the minor third. These intervallic distinctions, however, are external ones only; the vital qualities are defined as stated.

In thus designating the various degrees of chord-relation, I am simply stating incontrovertible scientific facts. It would, however, be utterly absurd to expect that the composer weighs all of these points and proceeds in mathematical agreement with them, in his writing; such a course, assuming it to be possible, could result in nothing but a lifeless mess. Then why, you ask, are these distinctions recorded? Because, *as general principles,* they are of indisputable validity. The composer's perception of them will, no doubt, be largely *intuitive;* "natural instinct" is the unimparted recognition of nature's laws and appointments, and the more normal and conscientious a person is, the more dependable will be his intuition. The classic masters possessed such normal musical instincts that they seem to have known, to have *felt,* without text books, what scientific research states in cold terms; and the proof of this rests in the indestructible charm that all sane music lovers sense and enjoy in their classic compositions—the absolute purity of their technic, the integrity of their methods, and the uncanny manner in which they approach and carry out the "natural" program.

Amplified and Inverted Forms

To return to our chords: by duplicating or inverting the intervals (chord-tones) many varied shapes are gained; and though these will naturally deport themselves in keeping with their environment, it must not be forgotten that *they all represent the same chord* and are all subject to the fundamental obligations of that chord. For instance, the chord of C may assume the following (and very many more) shapes:

Ex. 18.

The fifth and sixth of these clusters exhibit the omitted chordfifth (G). The chord-third (E) is very rarely omitted, and only for certain special (hollow) effects. The last two chords, in Ex. 18, differ more effectually (though not *radically*) from the preceding shapes, because the root (C) is not at the bottom; this so completely upsets the structure that such forms are called the first and second *inversions* of the chord (indicated by the Arabic numerals 1 and 2 beside the Roman numeral which always stands for the root-name of the chord). Any textbook discloses how they are handled.

The eighth of the foregoing chords is a rare form of the
I of C, with omitted root; it is possible, when so placed that its
surroundings confirm its identity as I. The omission of the root
of certain chords is legitimate and fairly common, as will be shown
later on.

Four-tone Chords

As a means of increasing the sonority and vitality of the
triads, they are often extended to include *four* tones by adding
another third at the top. This was first ventured, some three
centuries ago, with the dominant chord—in C major, the triad
G-B-D, to which an "upper story" F was affixed. The new tone,
F, being a seventh from the root, the 4-tone chord thus obtained
is called "chord of the seventh"—in this case, the dominant 7th,
or V^7 (five-seven). It must be well understood that merely
doubling a tone in a triad (as in Ex. 18), does not produce a
"four-tone chord." It must contain four different tones.

This process is applied to every tone of the scale, with the
following result:

Ex. 19.

Rare

IV₇ I₇ V₇ II₇ VI₇ III₇ VII₇

* The addition of a seventh to the tonic triad is rare, since the introduction
of so harsh and restless an interval robs the I of the very quality that is characteristic and essential—that of repose.

The most common of these four-tone chords are the dominant 7th (V^7), and the second-dominant 7th (the II^7).

The interval of a seventh pulls inward, as shown in Ex. 15,
in Chap. 2. Therefore, the 7th of the chord most commonly
moves *downward*.

Reverting to the somewhat curious process which we have
already referred to, and which is often applied to some of these
four-tone chords, it is now necessary to give it due consideration.
I refer to the *omission of the root*. This method of increasing
the flexibility of the chord by reducing its bulk and weight is
applied only to the two best chords, the V^7 and the II^7. If applied
to any of the others, it would (as can be instantly seen) simply
result in a quite different chord (triad). Thus, the V^7 of C major,
G-B-D-F, when deprived of its root, yields B-D-F—the chord
we have been calling the VII (Ex. 17), recognized from the start

as an illegitimate chord, without a perfect 5th, and standing, as "added" member, beyond the nucleus-members of the family. That the VII is really an "incomplete" dominant-7th chord is too obvious to justify doubt or discussion; in its sound, and in all of its movements, *it is identical with the dominant 7th.* (See Ex. 20, first measure.)

The case of the other one, the "incomplete" II⁷, seems a little different, but it is the same act and supported by the same proofs. *The sub-dominant triad (IV) is identical with the II⁷* in every technical sense. Early harmonists, beginning with Rameau (1683-1764) propounded the theory of the "chord with an added sixth," with direct reference to this very chord, our II⁷. But, while their intuition sensed the true harmonic relation, they placed the cart before the horse (see Ex. 20, second half).

Ex. 20.   Beethoven

V_7 Inc. V_7 *   II$_7$ Inc. II$_7$ or IV

*This chord (VII) is essentially the same without the G as it should be *with* it (as V⁷).

**The D is not an "added 6th," but is the actual root of the chord (II⁷); and instead of D being an "added" tone, it is the legitimate tone (root) which is *omitted* to form the triad F-A-C (the IV). This establishes the tonic chord as the actual basis and generator of the entire chord-family; there is no genuine root below it.

The first case, that of the VII, is, in my opinion, quite self-evident. Whereas the other one (the IV) does seem preposterous at a first glance, in view of its simplicity, its frequency and apparent independence, and also the deeply rooted prejudice that has been created by its evident close affinity with the tonic chord; so that the skeptic is hard to convince. Still, strict logic, fortified by every example of their use in classic music, proves that *the IV and the II⁷ are practically one and the same harmony.*

One interesting passage (key of A) from a Beethoven *Sonata* (*Op. 2, No. 2*) will suffice to substantiate this:

Ex. 21

I of A ——— | IV | V₇ ———
         | II₇ |

*The b, boldly accented, is the root of the chord.

Five-tone Chords

Similarly, and for the same purpose, still another third may be affixed at the top of a chord of the seventh, resulting in a five-tone chord.

Thus, with the V (G—B—D+F+A); the new tone, A, is a ninth (not a second, in this case) from the root; wherefore the chord is called "chord of the ninth."

This addition is made with the *five nucleus chords only;* and, as before, the tonic-9th is extremely rare, for the reasons already given; the VI^9 and III^9 are scarcely less so. The best five-tone chords are, as usual, the V^9 and II^9. And here, again, the omission of the root is far more common and consistent, since it reduces the unwieldy bulk, and brings the chord within an octave, without in the least jeopardizing the identity of the chord. It is applied *only* to the dominant and second-dominant 9th's—the incomplete V^9 is the VII^7, and the incomplete II^9 is the IV^7, both shown in Ex. 19.

All of these chords take exactly the same names and shapes in C *minor* as in C major; and, with very few exceptions, their movements are precisely as in major. The minor form of the incomplete V^9 (B—D—F—A♭) is the famous chord of the *diminished 7th*—famous for its loveliness, its dramatic flavor, and its well-nigh incredible flexibility: it moves, legitimately (according to its notations, its *sound* never changing) in no less than twenty-four directions, thus covering the entire range of keys—a metaphorical spinal cord of the tone-body. (See Chap. 10.)

No further chord-tones can be added; there are no six-tone chords in music. The notion of chords of the eleventh, thirteenth, and so forth, now happily obsolescent, is an aberration; for such additional "chord-tones" would so multiply the dissonant antagonisms as to flatly contradict the very essence of chord-formation, namely, *accord.* Such "combinations" (and very many more) do occur in practical composition, but they are only "combinations" of chord-tones and embellishing tones; and we shall find their true names when we come to the neighboring tones (Chap. 8). They are *not* "chords."

The Progressions of the Chords

With reference to the movements and intermingling of our family of chords, it is of prime importance to discriminate between the two opposite phases of motion, witnessed everywhere in nature: the *normal* movement, in obedience to the law of gravity; and the *imparted,* compulsive, coerced movements. To illustrate: I hold a brick in my hand; if I simply let go of it, it will drop to earth, as sure as fate; but, by applying force, I can make it fly upward or sidewise. Were it not for the operation of these two forces, we could build no houses: the imparted force lifts the material into its required place; the natural force (gravity) holds it there, giving stability to the structure. It is precisely the same with chords: they may move along the line dictated by nature, or they may be *forced* (gently, let us hope) to move in any direction the composer desires.

There are four different types or grades of movement from one chord into another: 1, repetition—all the tones common; 2, movement into a chord with two common tones; 3, movement into a chord with one common tone; 4, "foreign" progression, every tone changed. Thus:

"A" being an example of repetition, "B" of two common tones, "C" of one common tone, and "D" of "foreign" progression.

Of these (all of which are culled from Schubert) the first and third groups are *natural* (involuntary) movements; the second and fourth are *imparted* (voluntary) ones. Of particular significance is the third group, which I have called *normal* progressions, because they exemplify the action of gravitation. *If left to itself, the weight of a chord will carry it down, one perfect fifth, from root to root.* The III drops to the VI; the latter to the II; the II to the V, and so on. Starting thus at the top of Ex. 17, with the III, the chords roll normally down the series, towards the tonic—just as a ball rolls down a stairway until it strikes bottom. Thus (C major, normal progression):

* The most powerful and decisive move is, naturally, from dominant to tonic.

The apprehension of all these harmonic matters calls for no textbook; only in the event of putting them into practice will that be necessary.

But should the reader desire to investigate the choice and movements of chords, under limited conditions, he will find it easy enough, using simple compositions. For example; take the first eight measures of Beethoven's *Piano Sonata, Op. 2, No. 3* (in C major). The chords are placed thus:

Ex. 24

Rep.   Foreign Norm.

I   V   V₇   I   I   V₇   I   V₇   I   II₇   V   I
         Normal   Norm.

The ornamental (neighboring) notes are easily recognizable.

Good material for such a quest would be some book of church hymns, or college songs, the *Hallelujah Chorus* of Handel, and, later, the simpler "Songs without Words" of Mendelssohn, as well as Op. 68 of Schumann. One must be careful to follow changes of key, and must ignore all obvious ornamental tones.

SELF-TEST QUESTIONS

1. Define the derivation of our word "chord."
2. Define the formation of the Chord.
3. What is a Triad, and what are its three tones called?
4. How are the chords named, and how is their relative importance in their key determined?
5. Name the order of their importance.
6. How may a chord be amplified, and how is it "inverted"?
7. How are four-tone chords obtained?
8. Define the process of omitting the Root. To which *two* 4-tone chords is it limited?
9. How are five-tone chords obtained?
10. Which two of these may be "Incomplete?"
11. Name the four types of movement from one chord to another.

CHAPTER 4

How, and Why, Scale-steps Are Sometimes Altered

Constant adherence to the seven tones of the scale, as fixed by natural law, incurs a certain kind of monotony; just as too much of anything, no matter how good and essential it in itself is, may become irksome, tiresome. It is all well enough to travel the beaten track—to stay on the road—but an occasional excursion into byways brings new impressions, the delight of variety, and actually widens the sphere of action. And, if guided and limited by common sense, it can do no possible harm.

Origin of Altered Scale-Steps

Long ago, at so remote a period that historians cannot fix the starting point, players, and even more often, singers, appear to have inserted foreign (chromatic) tones between the scale-tones. Probably the first such foreign tone was an f-sharp (in the motive c-d-e-f-f♯-g), touched in gliding the voice from f to g. This was so easy and effective a method of introducing "color" and a sort of tentative emotional expression into their primitive vocal strains, that one need not wonder at its formal adoption and its gradual extension to other spaces of the scale, until a full chromatic scale of twelve tones was obtained. A similar result, from sliding the fingers along a string, or dragging the voice, is witnessed in the music of present-day Hindoos, and Orientals generally.

These primitive chromatic ornaments were at first accidental or instinctive. In time, their positive value was recognized, and their use became intentional and systematic, until, at present, in the theoretically established usages of modern music, they are accepted as extremely important factors of musical speech. They are accounted for as *chromatic alterations* of certain scale-steps, upward or downward—or, in some cases in both directions—and they take the formal appellation of *altered scale-steps* (glance at Ex. 25).

This name must be accepted in its exact grammatical meaning —the noun indicates the primary, fundamental object concerned— the scale-step; and the adjective, in keeping with the function of that part of speech, qualifies the primary object as *altered*, that is, chromatically raised or lowered.   This inflection does not change the *letter-name* of the scale-step, does not necessarily alter the key, and therefore does not affect the correlation of the steps (as illustrated in our first chapter). A scale-step is a scale-step, whether or not it be "altered" in the manner we are endeavoring to explain; and these particular chromatic inflections do not undermine the essential attributes of the scale-steps involved.

For example: the tone f-sharp, if placed in connection with tones that *unmistakably identify the key of C major,* is a raised 4th scale-step, not a specific f-sharp, but "f-sharped," so to speak. In order to be this, I repeat, it must occur in obvious C major surroundings; for if the f-sharp appears in surroundings which clearly locate the key of G major, it is not an "altered" step, but the legitimate 7th step of G; or, if in D major, the legitimate 3rd step.

The Chromatic Scale

Thus, the altered steps are responsible, as stated, for the chromatic scale.   All chromatic scales *sound* alike, regardless of key, inasmuch as this scale is created by dividing the octave into twelve exactly equal half-steps (by the universal adoption of equalized temperament) ; hence, the result must be the same, from any tone up or down to its octave.   But on the other hand, each chromatic scale differs from the others *in its notation,* and this— the notation—depends entirely upon the key in which the scale occurs, that is, upon the *key-note.*   For illustration, in the key of C major:

Ex.25

The tones with accidentals are altered scale-steps.   This notation seems to confirm the old rule that ascending chromatics are written with sharps and descending ones with flats. But this rule is valid only in a general way; it cannot apply to F-sharp Major, which cannot possibly have any flats ; nor to G-flat Major, which can have no sharps.   As declared above, the notation must depend upon the *key,* and must be determined by the laws which regulate the process of alteration. This brings us to the main question: Which steps of the scale may be altered, and in which direction? For this is not an arbitrary haphazard proceeding, but a strictly scientific one.

Where and How Alterations Are Made

It is obvious, first of all, that chromatic alterations can be made only between those scale-steps which lie a *whole step* apart; there can be no alterations between steps 3-4 or 7-8, since these are half-steps, with no intermediate tone. Thus c-sharp (or d-flat) may be inserted between c and d; in C Major it will be c-sharp, the *raised first step;* in A-flat Major it will be d-flat, the legitimate 4th step, followed by d-natural, the *raised 4th step.* In Ex. 25, c-sharp is the raised first step; d-sharp is the raised second step; f-sharp the raised 4th, and so on. In the descending form, b-flat is the lowered 7th step, a-flat the lowered 6th, and so forth.

The striking exception to the "old rule" occurs at the * in Ex. 25, where the raised 4th step (f-sharp) appears, instead of the expected g-flat. The unchallengeable reason for this is that there can *never* be a g-flat in the family of C—as will be shown directly. Make no mistake here. I do not deny that g may be followed by g-flat; but it can never happen *as long as the key remains C.* To make this clear, it is necessary to define the list of chromatic alterations; and for that purpose we must here again revert to the fundamental arrangement of the scale tones (the members of the key-family) given in our first chapter (the chain of perfect-5th links). The following presents the Key of C:

The logical application of a clearly defined natural law leads to the following conclusions: the lower three tones, F, C and G, are never chromatically *lowered* (in the key of C, be it well understood), since they are at the lower end of the chain. This is self-evident, as regards the f and the c, both of which are followed, downward, by the half-step spaces in the scale, which do not admit of a chromatic insertion; and, as to the g, the lowering of that tone would result in g-flat, which, as intimated above, is obviously too foreign to the key of C to be tolerated in that tone-community.

Similarly, the uppermost two tones, e and b, cannot be chromatically *raised,* not only because they are at the upper end of the chain, but because of the half-step space above them in the scale. The tone a, next below these two, may be raised, but it is rarely done.

On the other hand, quite logically, the lower three tones are readily and frequently *raised* and the upper three as readily *lowered.* And, as concerns the remaining central tone of the chain, d, it may be either raised or lowered. This apparently confusing, though entirely consistent, array of "alterations" is simplified by a diagram like the following:

Ex.27

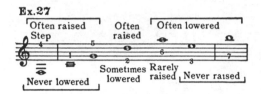

Probably the most frequent of all these chromatic alterations is the *lowering of the 6th scale-step;* though the raising of the 4th step is scarcely less common. The 2nd step is often raised, but only in major (for obvious reasons—d-sharp would be impossible in C Minor, which has the e-flat) ; and steps 2 and 4 are frequently raised together (Ex. 28, C). Step 2 is quite frequently lowered in minor, more rarely in major (Ex. 31, C and F, last chords). Step 5 cannot be raised in minor, since g-sharp cannot replace a-flat. Step 7 is lowered principally in minor, but may be lowered in major if followed by the lowered 6th step (Ex. 28, D). Step 6 is rarely raised, and almost invariably step 1 will be raised at the same time (Ex. 29).

All of this applies, by *scale-step number,* to every key, of course.

Many of these points will be more fully elucidated when we take up the minor mode, in our next chapter.

Now it is time to see how these alterations appear in authoritative examples. "A" and "B," in the following, are taken from Mozart's "Jupiter Symphony" (key of C) ; "C" from Liszt's "Les Préludes" (key of C) ; "D" from Brahms' "Symphony No. 4" (key of E) ; and "E" from Verdi's "Aida" (key of F).

For convenience, the signs plus and minus will be used to indicate the raised and lowered steps, respectively. Thus +2 signifies the raised 2nd step, —6 the lowered 6th step, and so on.

Ex. 28

These examples, picked at random, do not include all of the listed alterations; but the principal ones, the raised 4th step, lowered 6th and raised 2nd, are represented; here and there are

two simultaneous alterations.   Note the simple formation of the
melody (uppermost line) in group E; almost every tone is taken
from the tonic chord of F.   (Glance also at Ex. 41.)

The best way to gain full comprehension of the effect of these
altered scale-steps is to play the examples *without using the accidentals*—that is, with the unaltered, legitimate steps; it will thereby be clearly revealed how effectively they contribute to the charm,
richness and smoothness of the tone-fabric.

It will be felt, plainly, that these "alterations" contribute the
quality that might be called "color" to the melodies and harmonies
of the key.   The seven original, fundamental steps of the natural
scale are independent, unaffected members of the Family, each
with its distinct "personal" qualities and definite degree of relationship to the others, but of that comparatively blank ("white")
complexion consistent with its quasi-official character.   But the
chromatic inflection, or alteration, at once imparts a certain emotional quality to the step, not in the slightest degree altering its
fundamental relations, but in some cases intensifying, and in other
cases changing, its melodic tendency, or direction.   Thus, the 4th
step (f in C major) naturally falls: when *raised* (f♯), it is almost
certain to ascend.   The keynote, c, has no melodic inclination, and
may move to any point in its key: when *raised* (c♯), it must
ascend, to d.

To the foregoing, I cannot refrain from adding two other
examples, both from Beethoven, so striking and original, so characteristic of that greatest classic master of tone, as to assume very
peculiar significance; both passages are so arresting that we need
not be surprised at the caustic criticism they evoked, at that time.
The first is from Beethoven's Violin Concerto in the key of D:

Ex. 29.

The last measures show how Beethoven, later on, illuminates and justifies, in full harmony, his cryptic purpose.

The second is from his Symphony No. 8, keys of C and F:

Ex.30
Allegro

This gloriously audacious c-sharp stands exactly at the angle where C Major switches over into F Major, and is therefore at first the raised first step and then the raised 5th step. It is also "audacious," though far less glorious, to criticize Beethoven's notation; but it is conclusive, from its progression, that this is really d-flat—the lowered 6th step of F Major. Now, surely no one could sense the difference between c-sharp and d-flat more infallibly than Beethoven could, and I am thoroughly persuaded that Beethoven *meant* c-sharp—as usual, meant just what he said. The comparatively improbable, extraneous c-sharp (in both C and F Major), left "hanging in the air" without its compulsory progression upward to d, achieves precisely the grotesque effect at which Beethoven aimed.

The Altered Chords

The foregoing examples illustrate, almost exclusively, the comparatively superficial use of altered scale-steps, as transient ornaments of the *melodic* lines, without exerting any marked pressure upon the harmonic body as a whole—something after the manner of the cosmetics on milady's dresser, designed to beautify the surface of things. But the alterations may penetrate deeper, and be so applied as to modify or deflect the *chords,* thus affecting the entire harmonic scheme. The results of this broader application are known as *altered chords.*

The term implies the necessary limitations—an altered chord is not an altered *key,* but a deflection or ornamentation of the chord, strictly within the domain of its key.   Now, every chromatically altered scale-tone does apparently step outside of the key of that scale, and, consequently, every such "alteration" does establish a brief contact with some neighboring key.   But they should always confirm the principal key, and not that one to which the altered tones are peculiar.   In a word—if "one swallow does not make a summer," it is equally plausible that one chord does not make a (new) key.   There *are* instances where a single chord, from sheer weight, or length, or isolated importance, does represent its own key.   These will be considered when we come to our chapter on modulation.

Tendencies of Altered Steps

As to the progression of an altered scale-step, it is natural that all raised steps should ascend, and lowered ones descend; there are a very few exceptions which will be explained as they occur.

A few illustrations will suffice to acquaint the reader with the appearance of these altered chords in classic composition.

A is from Beethoven's Sonata, Op. 31, No. 2; B is from Weber's *Freischütz;* C is from Brahms' First Symphony; D the same; E from Brahms' 4th Symphony; F from the same; G is from Grieg's *Peer Gynt;* H from Wagner's *Rheingold;* I from Mozart.

Note the changes of key; all are marked.

These examples do not cover the ground, by any means. The more common alterations are purposely omitted; the reader can find a host of them himself, easily, on the pages of classic music.

The last one of the above examples ("I") contains a very common irregularity, in that the raised tones descend—that is, they are *pushed* down. See also, Example 25*; and Example 28, "B" and "E." This was an extremely favorite progression, almost a "mannerism," of Mozart's.

Here again, the only way to appreciate fully the effect and significance of these altered tones is to play the examples *without the accidentals.*

A few general facts bearing upon the choice of chords in which alterations are most likely to occur, may be welcome. The lowered 6th step appears very frequently in major, in dominant chords (in the VII₇ it results in the famous diminished-7th chord); in all second-dominant chords, and sometimes in the VI. The raised 4th step can occur *only* in second-dominant chords (*IV, II, II₇, IV₇*) both major and minor; in major, the raised 2nd step often accompanies the raised 4th step. The raised 5th step occurs only in tonic chords, in major. The following is in the key of C (major or minor):

Ex. 32
C Major: Lowered 6th step.

V₉   VII₇   II   II₇   IV₇   I   VI

C Major: Raised 4th, or 2d and 4th.
and

IV   II   II₇   IV₇   I   II   II₇   I

*Minor: Raised 4th.   Lowered 2d (Min. and Maj.)
or

IV   II₇   IV₇   I   II₁   I   II₁   V₇

* These four of the above altered chords in minor have historic nicknames: Italian 6th, French 6th, German 6th and Neapolitan 6th respectively. Nicknames are sometimes illuminating and convenient, but in this case their origin and appropriateness are somewhat dubious, and of absolutely no technical consequence.

N. B. All of these chords are followed by the tonic chord, or by the V₇ of their key.

The reader, or student, who desires more explicit information about the altered chords will find all the details in my "Tone-relations" and "Material."

SELF-TEST QUESTIONS

1. How did the practice of altering certain scale-steps originate?
2. To what scale do the chromatic alterations give rise?
3. Upon what must the notation of chromatic tones depend?
4. At which points in the natural scale are "alterations" impossible?
5. Which steps are never lowered; which ones never raised?
6. Which are the most common alterations?

7. What is the effect of these alterations upon the melodies and harmonies of the key?
8. What is an "Altered Chord"?
9. How do altered scale-steps move, normally?
10. Mention the most common irregularity; with which great master is it chiefly identified?
11. Which chords always follow an altered chord?

CHAPTER 5

How We Get the Minor Mode

All the operations of musical composition are performed upon one of two opposed basic platforms—either the major scale (or mode) or the minor scale (or mode). The 1st Symphony of Beethoven is evolved out of the mode of C Major; his 5th Symphony out of the C minor mode.

The major mode is *natural;* that is, it is determined by unalterable natural laws. The minor mode is *artificial,* a modification of the major mode in which nature acquiesces, since the changes are so simple and reasonable that they do not contravene any of her laws.

Major is divine, serene, dignified, inherently unimpassioned and therefore suited to the expression of lofty, heroic, forceful, dispassionate ideas. Minor is human, the consequence of an impulse to provide a medium appropriate for the expression of human passion, emotional fervor, dramatic feeling. Major is light; minor is dark, or sombre. In our musical experiences they stand for sunshine and shadow. And just as we enjoy most those days in which sunshine and shadow alternate, so, in music, we find wise composers relieving the predominant major brightness by occasional contrasting minor hues, and, in minor movements, similarly alternating with inspiriting major passages.

The Same Thing in Different Lights

From this it is evident that the major and minor modes are, in their external arrangement and effect, directly opposed to each other. But at the same time, they are *in all essential and fundamental respects identical with each other,* two contrasting aspects of the self-same object. For illustration—every individual technical operation, every mental action, every consideration of structure is determined on precisely the same principles in the composition of a minor symphony as in that of a major one; barring a very few details that concern merely the melodic movements, the technical treatment is exactly the same.

So we encounter, in the two modes, another striking example of the great underlying principle of all art (and all nature): that

53

of variety in unity: unity, conformity, in every *technical* (objective) respect; and variety of the most pronounced type in all external and *emotional* (subjective) qualities. To appreciate this most fully, it is but necessary to play any minor sentence (say, the first few measures of Beethoven's Fifth Symphony) in *major*— as if the signature were that of C major, instead of the prescribed three flats; this does not involve any changes in the arrangement of the notes, but it does evoke a totally different emotional picture —like the effect of a landscape on a bright sun-lit day, as compared with the same view on a rainy day, every object the same but imbued with a completely transformed complexion or mood.

The True Origin of Minor

The true origin of the minor mode has always been an object of study, conjecture and hypothesis, and numerous explanations have been suggested by sagacious students. Among these there are three theories which have arrested attention and invited credence, and it is no more than fair to present these, briefly, to the reader, before proceeding to the one which I have advocated, and which, despite apparent open controversy, seems to have been tacitly accepted, in a rather lukewarm (I believe, *intuitive*) fashion, all down the ages.

Three Theories of the Origin of Minor

The theory which, in view of its profoundly learned, mathematical nature, deserves first mention, is the hypothesis, sponsored by Hugo Riemann and other acute minds, that the minor mode is the *reverse* of the major—roughly stated, that minor is major upside down. It is true that the minor form has, almost throughout, the same intervals, serially, as the major, but beginning in the middle (at the tone *d*) and proceeding downward, along the chain of perfect fifths. This is, to say the least, an interesting conception; but one finds it hard to believe that nature actually planned so ingenious a scheme for the *genesis* of minor; it is probably no more than a coincidence, which corroborates in a delightful manner the omnipresent Unity of Nature. It must not be overlooked, moreover, that there are three distinct forms of the minor scale, to only one of which (the descending melodic form) this theory can be applied, while it loses most of its validity when referred to the other two, equally important, forms of minor. There is an apparent coincidence here: in Chap. 2 you have read that "every minor interval is the inversion of a major one" (minor intervals are major ones upside down). But this refers to *Intervals only,* and has nothing to do with the origin of the minor scale.

A second theory—that our minor is derived from the Aeolian mode of the Gregorian system of scales—is founded upon another "coincidence," but has nothing to do with the *origin* of minor. One has but to reflect what a singularly naïve notion it was that led to the accidental formation of the Gregorian modes—that of simply following the (for example) C major scale through an octave beginning at different steps, the Aeolian beginning at the 6th step, and running from *a* to *a* (along the white keys of the keyboard). See Ex. 1, Chap. 1. It *was* a clever idea; and the uses to which the various modes were applied in ecclesiastic music were so masterly, of such profound ingenuity, of such unexpected, novel, often overpowering beauty, that one cannot withhold admiration and veneration of them. And yet, it must be admitted that this clever notion was something of a childish game, rather than the issue of profound intellectual insight. And why should just the Aeolian mode be singled out as the significant prototype of a factor so prodigiously important in all modern music as our minor? And here, again, the coincidence applies to only one of the three forms of minor.

A third notion, a truly mischievous and deplorably misleading one, is that A minor (for example) is *derived* from C major. So deep-rooted is this utterly erroneous idea that it is very widely adopted as the best means of "explaining minor" to the young student. There is herein a faint analogy to the "Aeolian" theory; for that mode *was* derived (just as were all the other modes) from the fundamental extended hexachord system of Guido of Arezzo, corresponding to our major.

Resemblance Without Relationship

It is perfectly obvious and easily demonstrated that *every one* of these Gregorian modes is accounted for, in modern theory, by the system of altered scale-steps; therefore, by the way, we lose nothing by abandoning the old names. And to ascribe the *origin* of any scale to any other different scale is absolutely illogical; for the scales are separate entities and cannot be juggled or confounded at will. C major is the key of *C,* and A minor is the key of *A;* fundamentally they have nothing more to do with each other than that they are both members of the same tonality (family of keys). There will be more or less close resemblance, just as different individuals have been known to resemble each other to an embarrassing extent; but resemblance is not identity.

The key of A minor can no more be thus *identified* with C major than can one letter of the alphabet be confounded with another, with impunity or with reason.

Nor is there any sense in declaring that the minor mode "begins with the 6th step (of major)," for every key begins with its *first* step, its tonic or keynote, which, in the case of the key of A is *A*, whether the mode be major or minor.

In all of these hypotheses we have to do with nothing more important than coincidences—not tangible proofs, but mere coincidences, such as we should naturally expect to encounter between members of the same family, coincidences that point to the unity of nature's workings, wherein all the subtle subcurrents of tonal order and obligation seem to tend in the same direction.

The fact that all three of the foregoing hypotheses deal with one and the same form of our minor mode—the descending melodic form—might seem to assign greater significance to this form than to the other forms of minor; but the only fact that appears to substantiate this is that this form is linked with an important *melodic* principle—as will be seen; and melody is, so to speak, the "Lady of the House," to whom all must defer.

Minor, as a Modified Form of Major

If we have grasped the conception that the major and minor modes are *fundamentally* identical, simply two contrasting aspects of the same object, our deduction will be that one of them must be a modification or alteration of the other—and since major comes first, as the primary, natural form, it follows inescapably *that the minor is a modified form of the major.* And this, I am absolutely convinced, is the simple solution of the problem, so simple that our learned students have partly overlooked it and have peered beyond and beneath it, straining their eyes for an explanation more worthy of the problem; its very simplicity seems to have stood in its way.

The Alterations That Result in the Minor Mode

This modification of major, resulting in the minor form, is based upon the practice of *alteration*—the alteration of certain scale-steps by chromatically raising or lowering the pitch, by accidentals, without changing the letter-name. This device, one of the most effective in composition, and an extremely common one, was the subject of our preceding chapter; the reader who desires complete understanding of the origin of minor would do well to review that chapter.

The scale-steps involved in the formation of the minor mode, are, primarily, *the third and the sixth,* both of which are *lowered,* chromatically, from their position (pitch) in the major scale.

The momentous distinction between the act of alteration in this case, and the numerous alterations recorded in our preceding chapter is that there they were usually brief, *transient,* designed to embellish single melody tones or enrich certain chords; whereas here the alterations are *permanent.* Most of the scale-steps can be altered momentarily, but some of these alterations are so legitimate and plausible that they may extend through the entire sentence or the entire movement; hence, a whole symphony in minor. The third and sixth steps belong to this class, and the constant alteration (downward) results in that significant change in complexion which we call the minor mode. As stated above, and as everyone feels, the minor mode is more "emotional" than the major. And this is precisely because it results from the practice of *Alteration.* Compare this with our statement in the preceding chapter, between Exs. 28 and 29, defining the "colorful" influence exerted through Alteration.

A Tendency to Alter

Why these two particular steps submit so readily to the process of downward alteration is readily fathomed. The lowering of the third and sixth steps gives rise to no radical disturbance or embarrassment of the *harmonic,* and melodic, functions of the tones; whereas all the other altered steps do, to a greater or lesser degree, distort the chords, and sometimes interfere with the natural melodic movements. For example: the raised first step transforms the IV into an augmented chord, and the I into a diminished one. But the lowering of the sixth step simply changes the dominant chord from a major to a minor ninth, and the IV from a major to a minor triad; and that accounts largely for the extremely frequent use of the lowered sixth step in all styles of music, not excepting that of the great classic masters, Haydn and Mozart and especially Beethoven and Brahms. Further, the lowering of the third step has no other effect than changing the tonic chord from a major to a minor triad. (How inconsequential the exchange of major and minor *intervals* is, was shown in our second chapter. Review Ex. 9 and context.)

In fact, so natural and harmless are these two alterations that it seems as if they must have been made instinctively, from the beginning; minor is not "derived," in a subordinate sense, from anything; it is an independent, self-sufficient musical factor, coexistent and coördinate with major; it is quite likely that Adam, when moved to serenade Eve, did so with the emotional warmth that is peculiar to the minor mode—quite unintentionally, of course.

The Harmonic (or True) Minor Mode

Our definition, then, is: *the minor mode results from chromatically lowering the third and sixth steps of the corresponding major scale.* And this primary product is called the *harmonic* form of the minor scale, because it is the one which determines the *harmonic* functions of the key. Thus the key of C, minor mode, and the key of A, minor mode, (-3 and -6 indicating the lowered third and sixth scale-steps) as follows:

Ex. 33
C minor, Harmonic form:

A minor, Harmonic form:

This is the *true* minor scale, true to its origin and its distinctive nature. It will be seen that it has the same form upward and downward.

The Melodic Forms of Minor

The other two forms of the minor scale are merely modifications (alterations) of this harmonic form; and while these ulterior changes are imperative, they are so reasonable and appropriate that they are recognized as necessary, in civilized music. Since they are made for exclusively melodic reasons, they are known as the *melodic* forms of the minor scale.

The alterations are easily accounted for: the harmonic form contains, between the sixth and seventh steps, the unnatural interval of an augmented second (in C minor, A-flat to B-natural, one-and-a-half steps) known as the "unsingable" interval, because, while singing A-flat, the mental ear cannot accurately locate so remote a tone as B-natural (nine links distant in the chain of perfect fifths). You may think you can sing it; and you can, approximately, though not without difficulty and discomfort. Now, in ascending, the B-natural may not be changed, because of its strong inclination to pass upward into the keynote; therefore in order to remove the awkward progression, the sixth step in *ascending* is raised from A-flat to A-natural (put back where it belongs, in major), and the scale is smoothed out to a normal succession of whole and half steps.   Contrariwise, in descending, since the A-flat has an equally strong tendency to pass downward to the dominant (and therefore should not be altered), the seventh step, in *descending,* is lowered from B-natural to B-flat.   Thus in the key of C (minor mode): A is the ascending melodic form, and B the descending melodic form—

Note that only the *upper half* of the scale is involved; the lower half is the same in all three minor forms, because *the lowered third step is the distinctive unit of the minor mode,* under all circumstances.   For instance, in the key of C, the e♮ invariably establishes the *major* mode, while e♭ confirms some one of the *minor* forms.   Thus:

*An example of this peculiar form may be seen in Ex 28, D (Brahms, E major, alto and soprano parts).

Ex. 35 illustrates the legitimate ascending and descending forms; but they are sometimes used in the opposite directions, for purely *harmonic* reasons; thus, when the *dominant* harmony is present, the B-natural (in C minor) cannot well be altered, and therefore the "raised" sixth step will go with it, whether the scale runs upward or *downward.*   And when the harmony is evidently *subdominant,* the A-flat cannot well change, and B-flat must join it, whether the direction is downward or *upward.*   Thus, in the following, key of C (minor mode):

in A the ascending form runs downward, and in B the descending form runs upward.

The finest illustrations of correct treatment of these various forms of the minor scale are to be found, naturally, in the music of Bach. The following examples are gleaned from the C-sharp minor *Prelude* in Book I of his "Well-Tempered Clavichord":

Ex. 37

It will be seen that here the B-natural and A-natural (lowered form) are *always placed together;* and the same is true of the

A-sharp and B-sharp (raised form), the choice depending upon melodic or harmonic conditions.

The harmonic form, with the "unsingable" interval, can of course be *played* without compunction, on any instrument; and it is not infrequently used, in instrumental music, for its unusual weird effect. It is a strikingly common feature of Hungarian, Turkish and all Oriental music. Beethoven is by no means averse to its employment, and even in Bach's instrumental works it is sometimes encountered. In all vocal music, however, it is rare. Examples of its use occur in (a) Beethoven, Op. 90 (key of E, minor mode), (b) in scale passages, and (c) in a broken diminished-seventh chord:

One particularly instructive example of the use of minor is worth adding. It is from the D-flat Mazurka of Chopin (Op. 30, No. 3), and the reader would do well to consult the original—the last seventeen measures:

The first four-measure phrase, clearly in D-flat major, is *repeated,* with the lowered third and sixth steps, clearly in D-flat minor. The closing chord returns to major. The eight measures which precede these, in the original, are still more interesting: measures one to four are clear major; measures five and six (a repetition) contain the lowered sixth step only—therefore it is still major; measure seven restores the sixth step to its proper place; measure eight repeats this measure, again with the lowered sixth step. The relation of minor to its *corresponding* major is here incontestably demonstrated. Similar examples of the exchange of the modes, during repetitions, are very common in the music of Schubert, Mozart and other masters.

The Signatures of the Minor Keys

Only the major keys have distinctive signatures. The minor keys, which are not *natural* scales but *artificial* ones, are therefore obliged to borrow a signature from one of their major associates; and the procedure that is adopted in the choice of a signature for the minor key is dictated solely by the consideration of *convenience,* that major signature being selected which most nearly coincides with the accidentals present in the minor scale. In the case of C minor, for instance, the signature of three flats is chosen, because, first of all, it contains the indispensable E-flat (third step) defined above as being the distinctive mark of the minor mode; and besides this it accounts for the A-flat (sixth step). Hence the rule that a minor key adopts the signature of the major key *upon the third step of the minor scale.* Thus (C minor, 3 flats):

Ex.40

(key of C, minor-mode) ; the accidental, B-natural, must not be confounded with those accidentals which, in our preceding chapter, recorded the raising or lowering ("alteration") of certain scale steps. The lowering of the sixth and third steps here—in C minor —is indicated by two of the flats in the chosen signature; and the presence in the latter of one flat more than is needed, necessitates the natural (before B, in this case) to cancel the effect of that superfluous flat.

SELF-TEST QUESTIONS

1. Define the contrasting attributes of Major and Minor.
2. In what respect are they nevertheless identical?
3. What three theories have been advanced concerning the origin of the minor mode?
4. What is probably the most plausible and trustworthy theory of its origin?
5. Which scale-steps are affected, and in which direction?
6. Why may the 6th and 3rd scale-steps be lowered, permanently, without affecting the key?
7. Define the Harmonic form of minor.
8. Define the two Melodic forms, and the manner in which they are accounted for.
9. What is the "unsingable" scale-interval?
10. Which signature does a minor key use?

CHAPTER 6

The Facts, and Mysteries, of Melody

Of all the strange and apparently unfathomable things that happen, in the utterances and revelations of the spirit of tone (and there are very many such), none seems enshrouded in deeper mystery than the element of melody. Some phases of it, probably the most vital and essential of melody's attributes, have baffled us all our lives; and we admit frankly that no angle of musicology seems so mystery-laden, so inscrutable, to us, after a long lifetime of earnest pondering, as that of melody.

Melody is defined, prosaically, as *any succession of single tones.* This is easy to understand. But it is by no means easy to discriminate judicially between immortal melodies, and good, bad and indifferent melodies. Some outstanding conditions of good, acceptable melody are quite obvious: the succession of tones should be reasonably *related* to one another throughout the phrase or sentence; there should be recognizable *subdivision; balance* and *contrast,* as regards direction and rhythm; and there should be such architectonic traits as serve to create a clear aggregate impression of the entire "moving" tone-picture. This goes without saying.

The Elusive Spirit

But what is the secret force that, while uniformly conforming to these exterior conditions, moulds the melodies of each one of the great composers in a distinctive form peculiar to that particular musical spirit, so that we unerringly recognize this type as Beethoven, that as Mozart, this as Schubert, that as Chopin, and so forth, through the whole range of melodic conception? It is a differentiation far more subtle than the traits which characterize the poetic or prose effusions of Shakespeare, Tennyson, Shelley or Kipling; for these are rather distinctions of *style* than of spiritual contents. And how, with all their individuality, does some mysterious instinct place the whole line of tones *just so,* so firmly that the alteration of one single tone may completely transform the message—invariably to its harm?

I recall one instance: while playing a four-hand version of

a Beethoven quartet with a friend, my right hand shot beyond
the mark and accidentally struck a melody note one tone above
its proper place; the result was so ludicrous that we both burst
into laughter. Some such mishaps might be easily accounted for;
but many would remain inexplicable and merely confirm the
mysterious wisdom that traced the line exactly as though some divine will ordained it. "Why it should be so, with these elemental
single tones—but if one knew that, there would be no more mystery in music." (J. D. M. Rorke, "A Musical Pilgrim's Progress"). One can point out certain characteristics, both as concerns
the choice of tones and their rhythmic placing and proportions,
which stamp this melody as Scotch, that as Russian, others as
Italian, French or Negro; but the real difference lies far beneath
all such external elements; and that is the mystery of melody.

Melodies Born and Melodies Made

It is a widespread popular belief that melodies are conceived,
not made; that they come into being through some occult spiritual
impulse, commonly called "inspiration," and not as the sober
product of conscious planning and calculation. The truth lies, as
usual, midway between the two views, for both are no doubt to
some extent defensible. It is tempting, and affords a sort of
inspired consolation, to imagine the birth of a melody as an ema-
nation from some divine source; to envisage melody as arising
like the mist from the moist soil under the vivifying rays of the
sun and mounting to the sky to unfold in cloud-shapes of indescribable beauty and colors of ineffable loveliness. This, also,
seems to conceal a kernel of truth; for there *are* melodies that
we know and instinctively clasp to our musical bosom, melodies
whose origin we seem utterly unable to account for. But, on the
other hand, it is impossible to ignore or deny traits, in the great
majority of our finest classic melodies, which were placed there
in consequence of deliberate purpose and intellectual plotting.

Take, for example, the initial thematic phrase (the *Presto*)
of Mozart's *Overture* to "Figaro":

Ex.41   Presto

Even the most ardent admirer of Mozart would scarcely perceive any marked signs of "inspiration" in this melody. It is a fine line, unquestionably, traced with sureness by a master hand. But it is clearly the product of that deliberate purpose and mental selection of which I spoke above—a product of genius, to be sure, but the genius of applied wisdom, and not of lofty emotional impulse. Compare with this the first thematic phrase of Schubert's "Unfinished Symphony":

and the difference is deeply felt; here is the unfathomable mystery of inspiration; one is baffled in the attempt to scan the technical "design" or to define the synthesis of this wonderful phrase, according to any accepted tenets of melodic structure!

To avoid losing our heads at the very outset, we must take refuge in the assurance that there are a number of well defined and incontrovertible facts concerning melody which can be grasped and proven, and which afford us some tangible information and reliable guidance along the highway of the melodic Wonderland. These facts seem to have but little bearing upon the *conceptive* phases of melody (though I contend, stoutly, that their influence is nowhere escapable), but concern the *constructive* phases. And to these we must give first attention.

Natural Inclination of Scale Steps

One striking attribute of melodic conduct which is, in my opinion, of truly vital importance, has been treated, oddly enough, with complete indifference by musical theorists generally. I refer to the inherent bent or tendency of certain steps of the scale to move in a certain direction.

The seven tones of the natural scale are divided into two opposite groups; the one group consists of the 1st (and 8th), 3rd, and 5th scale steps, those which constitute the chord of the key and which share alike in that quality of *repose* which is the significant essence of the tonic harmony. The other four, steps 7, 6, 4, and 2, are, on the contrary, *active* in quality, and, precisely because they lie outside of the circle of rest, are automatically impelled, by the law of gravity, to fall back into this circle, each tone progressing to that one of the inactive steps *to which it lies nearest.* Thus, step 7 *ascends* to step 8, because it is nearer to 8 than to 5; step 6 *descends* to step 5, since it is nearer 5 than 8; step 4 *falls* to step 3, which lies nearer than step 5; step 2 is active, but, since it lies exactly equidistant from steps 1 and 3, it may move either up or down. For ilustration, note the following from Beethoven's Op. 2, No. 2 (B):

Ex.43

Each active scale step may move farther than one step (6 down to 4 and so forth), but as a rule the *direction* will be normal. Also, for harmonic reasons, the leap of a third, either up or down, is always correct; both of these conditions are shown in Ex. 43, C.

This is a vital melodic tendency, as fundamentally natural as the swing of a pendulum. It is the *regular* progression, and is obeyed in the great majority of cases. But nature is liberal; no "rule," and especially not this one, is hide-bound. There is a fairly large minority of cases in which the rule is set aside, and these constitute a class called *irregular* scale-progressions.

Irregular Progressions

To elucidate this point, we must recall a statement made in our third chapter, in reference to the "two phases of motion witnessed everywhere in nature: the *normal* movements, in obedience to the law of gravity, and the *imparted,* compulsive movements." You may recollect the illustration of the brick; if released from the hand that holds it, it will drop to earth, as sure as fate; but, by applying *force,* it can be made to move upward or sidewise. This reasoning applies to the active steps of the scales: if permitted to follow their natural bent, step 7 will ascend, steps 4 and 6 will descend; but they may be *pushed,* along the scale, in the opposite direction. Thus, step 7, *if approached from step 8,* may (not must) proceed downward to step 6; step 6, if approached from step 5, may pass up to step 7; step 4, if preceded by step 3, may go on up into step 5. In other words, while the progressions 7 to 6, or 6 to 7, or 4 to 5, when taken *alone,* are "wrong," the total runs: 8-7-6-5, or 5-6-7-8, or 3-4-5 are perfectly feasible; and they are necessary, as a means of rounding out the entire octave-scale. For example, A, key of B♭, Beethoven, Op. *22*; B, Brahms, Intermezzo, Op. 117, No. 1:

The irregular progressions occur at each asterisk.

The natural tendency is strongest from the 7th step, upward, because of its close proximity to the 8th step, which attracts it, like a magnet. Step 6, downward, is a trifle less urgent in major, though equally strong in minor, and step 4 can quite easily be deflected. Step 2, as has been seen, is so non-committal that it exerts no force in the tone mechanism and is usually disregarded altogether as active tone.

This covers the ground of scale-step activity, and an extremely significant covering it is. The student may be amazed, in scanning any page of classic music, to see how very prevalent these natural movements of the active tones are, particularly in the *melodic* parts. For the true genius recognizes and bows to the decrees of nature; he seeks the truth; and every sane, normal perception falls in line with his methods, and experiences undisturbed enjoyment.

Let me not be misunderstood: no one could be less willing to impede progress than I am. But progress should be made in the right spirit and manner—not in defiance of the eternal laws of the universe. The progress that we witness from Haydn to Mozart, to Beethoven, to Wagner and Brahms, concerns *methods* only, a richer variety of interpretations and applications of nature's laws, a profounder sense of the potentialities of these laws, but never in rude, willful contradiction of them. Wagner widened the scope of modulation; Brahms struck deeper into the resources of counterpoint and structural formation; but *nowhere* can one point to a direct subversion or overstepping of the law, in the music of these progressive geniuses.

There are a few other "rules" of melody, but lack of space forbids their enumeration here. The author's book on "Melody Writing" defines them all.

Furthermore, the watchful student will encounter a few other irregularities and "exceptions," but they are so rare, in really good music, that they do not warrant special notice. The true master handles them in a way that is both skillful and loyal, and that contributes more to the mystery, than to the facts, of melody; the "popular" composer abuses them in a fashion that appears "original," and does create a certain glamour of "variety." But in doing so he undermines the stability and nobility of the genuine tone-structure.

Chord and Scale as Melodic Sources

Wherever the melodic succession does not pursue the line of the scale—that is, wherever there is a skip—some *chord* is involved. In truth, I question whether, ordinarily, melody derives from any other source than the chord. Wagner always fixes his harmonic scheme in the orchestra, and the melody (vocal part) threads its way through this scheme, at times in what strikes one as an "unmelodious," surely unusual, fashion. Although the influence of the scale is far more ancient than that of the chord, the underlying impulse, even in the most primitive song, is clearly supplied by the *Chord*. Thus, we witness countless examples of melodic motives and even whole phrases emerging straightway out of the tonic chord—for example, in the following: (A), Verdi, key of G; (B), Rubinstein, key of F:

The asterisk indicates tones "added" to the chord. See also: Beethoven, Symphony No. 3, measures 3-6; Symphony No. 4, measures 43-44; Symphony No. 9, measures 17-19; Brahms, Violin Concerto, principal theme; and innumerable other examples.

Of course, the dominant chord is drawn upon in the same

way, and, more rarely, the other chords of the key. Thus in Verdi's "Anvil Chorus" (key of G):

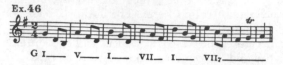

Ex.46

G I___ V___ I___ VII___ I___ VII₇_____

the chords are "broken"—just as the solid blocks of granite are broken, to provide units for the lines of our buildings.

The other great source of melodic progression is the *Scale*. For illustration, in Beethoven's Op. 59, No. 1 (key of C):

Ex. 47.

It is clear that the peculiar significance of this scale-melody (Ex. 47) lies in its *rhythmic* formation. Played in a uniform rhythm of quarter notes, it is as insipid as a scale exercise of Czerny. The accents and the lengthened notes place certain of the tones in a stronger light, illuminating them and deepening the shadow of the other tones—quite in the manner of a skillful elocutionist who by means of dynamic inflections can invest his sentences with overpowering appeal, or, on the other hand, if he chooses, can reduce them to gibberish. (See also, Ex. 44.)

Occasionally, the more emotional chromatic form of the scale is used, in alternation with the diatonic order. For example, in the following— (A) Saint Saëns, "Samson and Delila," (B) Mendelssohn:

Ex. 48. A.

E♭ I_____ II₇_____

B.

V₇___ A I_____

The reader will scarcely need to be told that it is not common for a melodic phrase to be limited exclusively to either the chord or the scale; the two forms (known as conjunct and disjunct motion) usually alternate with each other, as the most cursory glance will show.

Further, the coöperation of heart and mind (artless conception and technical manipulation) is witnessed in countless instances like the following—key of B minor, Beethoven, Op. 106:

in which a melodic motive is repeated, first appearing as involuntary conception, and then, by the application of will and intelligence, as artificial manipulation.

Melodic Idioms

Music has its idioms, or stereotype forms, as well as our languages have.   Probably the most ancient and primitive melodic impulse is the reiteration of a single tone, as the natural intuitive reaction of the human mind to simple bird-calls and other natural sounds. Thus (A) in Verdi's "Il Trovatore"; and (B) Beethoven:

Verdi was particularly prone to begin his melodic sentences as shown at (A).   See, also, Ex. 43, (B).

A remarkably popular melodic figure is the leap from step 5 to step 8, followed by the ascending scale; of this, a multitude of examples may be found, such as: (A) Beethoven's Symphony No. 2; (B) Mendelssohn's Symphony No. 3; (C) Schumann's Op. 68; (D) Brahms' Op. 79, No. 1; and (E) Mendelssohn:

Ex. 51

See also, *Lead, Kindly Light; The Long, Long, Weary Day; Oh Happy Day; How Dry I Am;* Beethoven, Op. 13, last movement; and so on indefinitely.

Besides these, there are some melodic idioms which trace their origin to national or racial influences. For example, the downward leap of a fourth, so characteristic of many Russian folk melodies. It is deftly utilized by Tchaikovsky in his string-quartet, Op. 11 (key of B-flat) thus:

Ex. 52.

and is salient in the famous *Volga Boat Song.*

Also there is the strong Scotch national flavor that attaches to their almost exclusive use of the five-tone scale (the five *nucleus* tones of the natural scale). For example, *Auld Lang Syne* (key of F):

Ex. 53

Only five scale tones are present here; the "added" 4th and 7th steps (B-flat and E) do not appear.

Everyone is familiar with the hearty, substantial quality of German folk-song, the smooth, engaging melodic flow of the Italian, the lively, snappy rhythms of the French, the weird, melancholy or veiled passion of the Oriental.

The reader whom these details may stimulate is urged to play his pieces henceforth with closer attention and seek to discover for himself the existence of these, and other, important traits of melody.

Melody as a Language

To summarize our impressions, this is as near as one can approach to a solution of the mystery of melody: music is a *language;* the melodies are the sentences; the tones are the words. Some human souls *know* this language, by intuition or natural endowment; others seem to be nearly or quite without a conception of it, as if it were Sanskrit or some other foreign tongue. He who possesses the knowledge can create melodies that are significant, impressive and beautiful. He who is ignorant of it, can, at best, echo what others have spoken (just as any one may "quote" Shakespeare), or write after a certain composer's style (as one apes the manner of Kipling). But in this latter case the results are weak, superficial, slangy or grotesque melodic sentences, devoid of real value, though possibly in a sense "attractive," calculated to tickle the taste of the public. Surely Beethoven understood and mastered the language of music. And surely there are some musically prophetic minds among the lowliest people who have an instinctive apprehension of the tone-language and can use it, when the impulse is felt. This explains the origin of national tunes and folk-songs generally; and this is why the latter are often so eloquent, so true, so searching, why their charm is universal, irresistible and enduring.

Musical Literacy

I repeat, the person who possesses a knowledge of the tone-language may produce really fine, original and important melodies; but, after all, it is what he *learns* by earnest study that enables him to make the best, most emphatic and effective use of his melodies. For music, like all languages, has its orthography, its grammar, its syntax and prosody; and these must be respected and properly handled, if the product is to be masterly and valuable.

Herein we recognize some of the *Facts* of melodic conduct. But the *Mystery* is undefinable: it consists not in any one thing, but in a host of subtle factors which intermesh and react upon each other so intricately that their exact analysis seems a hopeless task. Viewed from almost any angle, melody (or "music," which is the same thing) is a mystery. No one can say what these tone-words mean; there are no equivalents to them in any tongue on earth; and almost any endeavor to translate them, to define their "meaning" in terms of human speech and make them "tell a story," leads to the most childish, silly and utterly fruitless results. The impulse to do this is natural; we have a vague consciousness that the real meaning evades us, and we desire earnestly to fix it—just as we long to give a picture a title. We may manage to interpret the picture, for it presents tangible features; but with music we are all at sea and crave in vain some definite means of identification.

So we are bound to confess that melody remains a mystery. Some have a little knowledge of its language. Some have much. Many of us, I fear, have almost none. But there must be some chord in every human breast that vibrates in sympathy with the divine voice of music.

SELF-TEST QUESTIONS

1. What element of music is most mysterious?
2. Give the technical definition of melody.
3. What two opposite creative forces enter into the conception of melody?
4. Which three scale-steps possess the quality of repose, and why?
5. Which 4 scale-steps are active, and why?
6. Name the natural tendency of step 7; step 6; step 4; step 2.
7. How may these natural tendencies be counteracted, and which irregular progressions are correct?
8. Which are the two main sources of melodic succession?
9. Mention some of the idioms of melody.
10. To what do we compare music, as a medium of expression?

CHAPTER 7

THE VITAL FUNCTIONS OF RHYTHM IN MUSIC

Rhythm is the life-giving principle in music. If we liken harmony to the heart, and melody to the lungs, the element of rhythm may be compared to the muscular system of the musical organism, without which the body is paralytic, incapable of manifesting the energy within it. Rhythm vitalizes the entire sound-mass. Without rhythm, music would be something like the bronze statue of some celebrity, placed upon a pedestal as a reminder (good, as far as its inspiring influence goes) but unable to exhibit any physical activity and therefore comparatively valueless. But *with* rhythm the array of tones is electrified into manifold life and displays a complex of movements that are as arresting as they are vital and significant.

For music is a Moving Picture, one in which the successive impressions are conveyed to the mind through the ear; in which concrete audible lines of melody and the resonant harmony supply a parallel to the abstract, unreal, visionary persons and objects appearing on the screen.

Music is the most ancient example of this particular order of mental perceptions. It is as old as humanity itself, and it contributed to human entertainment ages unnumbered before that which is known in our day as the moving picture came into being.

A Non-Dimensional Art

It is impossible to hear a piece of music all at once; for this is a panorama of shifting sounds which strike successively upon the ear. In this respect music is totally unlike the arts of architecture and painting, in which latter the concept can be, and is, taken in completely at a glance. Hence music most closely resembles poetry and the art of literature, whose impressions are likewise presented in progressive succession. If the music does not move, it is dead, as dead as our bronze statue; and, in order to bring it to life, a multitude of physical operations are necessary—the motions of the hands on the keyboard or upon the instruments of the orchestra, or of the vocal cords and lungs of the singer. If instead of playing a composition, you sit back in your easy chair and read it (and hear it) with your eyes, you must train your vision upon the notes, and your eyes must *move* across the page, in order to recreate mentally the sounds represented by the musical symbols.

Now *rhythm,* in its application to music, is the factor that determines the method in which this progressive forward movement of the tonal picture is conducted—its speed, its alternate relaxing and speeding up, its pauses: in a word, the entire machinery of the moving picture.

Divisions of Time

For music is an art of *time;* not of *space.* And the amount of time that is consumed in the performance of the musical composition is divided, just as time is, everywhere, in the orderly operations of creation and in the regulated activities of humanity. The adopted time-units of day, hour, minute and second consequently dictate the division of the time-range of the music into phrases, measures, beats and their subdivisions. But these divisions of time, while they serve the same purposes of system and proportion, are not the quality that is known as rhythm; they are purely the mathematical basis from which all rhythmic distinctions are derived. What transforms this lifeless mathematical scheme into animated objects, *rhythm proper,* is the principle of *differentiation,* as will be pointed out further on.

The Beat

The first step, then, in the establishing of a rhythmic system in music, is the division of time into regular units of uniform length, which we call "beats." This name may be accounted for by the fact that, in ordinary moderate tempo (movement), these pulses correspond to our heartbeat, about seventy-two in a minute. In notation, the beat may be represented by a note of any time-value, though the quarter-note is by far the most common choice. The longest specimens on record occur in the first two studies of Clementi's "Gradus ad Parnassum" where the *whole-note* is chosen as beat (signature 3-1) and also briefly near the end of Saint-Saëns "Symphony in C Minor." And the opposite extreme is found in Beethoven's "Sonata, Op. 111," where the thirty-second note figures as beat (signature 12-32).

The tempo marks, *adagio, andante, allegro, presto,* and so forth, are supposed to refer to the beats; but this is not always

the case, since these terms often denote the character, rather than
the speed, of the phrases.

Thus, for instance, there are two entirely different kinds of
6-8 measure, a slow (normal), and a fast; in No. 18 of Mendelssohn's "Songs Without Words" the tempo mark, *andante con
moto,* surely refers to the beats, whereas in Nos. 3, 34 and 45 of
that work it as surely refers, not to the six beats, but to the two
accents; the effect is that of 2-4 measure, in triplet-division. The
same is true, of course, of 3-8, 9-8 and 12-8; compare No. 22
(Mendelssohn), the tempo defined by beat, with No. 26, the tempo
defined in triplets.

The Measure, Simple

The next act is the *grouping of these beats* in so-called measures. Since this results in the operation of differentiation, the
actual rhythmic distinction may be said to begin with this grouping process. For the consciousness of "grouping" is awakened
by differentiating the *force* of the beats, some being heavy and
others light.

Of these beat-groups there are only two kinds, the group of
two units (called duple meter) and the group of *three* beats (triple
meter). There can be no other form; every conceivable variety
of larger measure is simply compounded out of these two. They
are analogous to the only two kinds of lines in nature, the straight
line and the curved line; there are no other kinds.

Duple and Triple Meter

In duple meter each heavy pulse is followed by a light one;
in triple meter, two light strokes follow each heavy one. Hence,
duple meter is a *regular* alternation of one heavy and one light
pulse, while triple meter is an *irregular* alternation of one heavy
with two light beats. Thus, duple meter suggests the square, and
triple meter the circle; the general effect of the former is therefore
angular, four-square, whereas triple meter is smooth, graceful,
swinging (this is exemplified in the march and waltz respectively).
These rhythmic clusters exist, of course, in poetry also, and form
the basis of such lines as these:

duple: The | cúrfew | tólls the | knéll of | párting | dáy;
triple: For | wáys that are | dárk—and | trícks that are | váin;

The heavy beat is called the accent (v), and it must be the *first* beat, because it supplies the force with which a new thrust of the rhythmic piston is made—the power put forth to make each new start. In notation the measures are separated by so-called bar lines.

Compound Measures

But the measure is not always limited to these two, or three, original beats. It may contain four, six, nine, twelve or more; but these are never anything more than *multiplied forms of the simple measures*. It is needless, even foolish, to speak of "quadruple" meter, for the measure with four beats is simply the sum of two duple measures, the second bar line being omitted; and this intermediate bar line is only disguised, not destroyed: there is the inevitable accent on the *third* beat, just as if a bar line preceded it. And the same situation holds for all other, larger, compound forms (6-8, 6-4, 9-8, 12-16, and so forth).

Accentuation

The rhythm is "regular" when the accentuation (force of accent) falls, as it should, upon the first beat of each measure. And we must distinguish, sharply, the various methods by which accentuation is realized. There are "natural" accents and "artificial" ones: it is the natural accent which asserts itself, naturally, on the first beat of each metric group, and this is defined by counting *one*-two, or *one*-two-three.

The rhythm is "irregular" when, by any means, stress is laid upon *any other* than the first beat. Regular rhythm is so natural that it is accepted as a matter of course, and in the great majority of musical motives this sort predominates. But it is the irregular patterns that give birth to countless varieties of interesting rhythmic figures and completely remove the fatal menace of monotony. Therefore this is the most fruitful and fascinating field of all rhythmic life.

The question arises: how can an accent be shifted from its legitimate location at the *beginning* of each metric group? There are several ways. All rhythmic vitality, as stated before, begins with and persists in differentiation of one kind or another. In the original uniform metric groups there is the difference in *stress,* created by the alternate heavy and light beats, so that even when the phrase consists of strictly uniform notes (as in our *Yankee*

Doodle) one is impelled involuntarily to nod one's head or tap
with the foot, if only lightly, at each first beat (try to emphasize
any other notes in *Yankee Doodle* and you will see what I mean).

But this is only one of the methods of instituting differentiation; accent is determined, besides, by differences in the *length*
(time values) of the notes.   A longer note will, without fail, produce the effect of accentuation; and it is when the longer tones
stand in the expected place, at the beginning of each group, that
the rhythm is "regular."   For example, in Schubert's "Symphony
in C Major":

Ex. 54

the rhythm is regular, normal, since the longer notes stand upon
the accented beats.   There is, it is true, a very slight irregularity
in measures 2 and 3, 5 and 6, where the second accent (third beat)
is just a trifle heavier than the first one; but this is negligible.
See also the thirty-seventh "Song Without Words"; the rhythm
is perfectly regular throughout, only excepting measure 35, in
which the syncopating tie gives undue length to the fourth six-
teenth-unit.

On the other hand, the following melodies (*A*, Dvorák's
"Symphony from the New World"; *B*, Schubert's Op. 94, No. 4;
C, Beethoven's Op. 18, No. 4; *D*, Beethoven's Op. 59, No. 1) all
betray the delightful traits of irregular rhythm—not "wrong,"
mind you:

Ex. 55

At *A*, the second longer note falls on the *second half* of the
third beat, instead of on the beat itself; this throws an unexpected

"accentuation" upon the normally light sixth 8th-note of the measure. Note that the irregular rhythm occurs *twice,* in successive measures. It is a very important unwritten law in music (perhaps everywhere) that any irregularity is justified by persistence or repetition; for such insistence shows that it is a deliberate intention, not a blunder. This, however, applies only to reasonable "irregularities," not to downright errors. An isolated irregularity is confusing, whereas its restatement restores the balance and makes the unusual outlines clear and acceptable.

At *B,* the second 8th-beat, which should be very light, becomes heavy by the undue length of the note; the effect is so confusing that one would (in listening, not seeing) assume that the bar line *followed* the two 16th-notes. This peculiar rhythm persists constantly during fifty-two measures. *C* and *D* are similar; the second beat receives the stress that pertains normally to the first beat. This method of producing artificial accentuations by means of longer notes might be called *metric,* inasmuch as it is a question of time-values.

Another method of locating the stronger pulses consists in changing the chord at the proper accents; by this means the "new" chord confirms the impression of a "new" group—a method we may call the *harmonic.* When the change of harmony takes place at the bar line, thus marking the natural accent, the rhythm is regular; if made at any unaccented point, it is irregular. For illustration: *A* (Beethoven, Op. 18-4); *B* (Beethoven, Op. 74); *C* (Chopin, Op. 12).

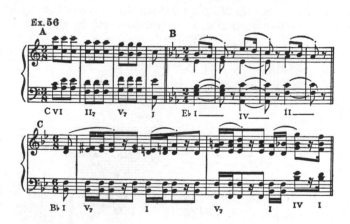

The rhythm at *A* is regular, because the change of chord occurs at the accent, thus confirming its natural location. At *B* it is irregular, since the changes are made at the unaccented second beat, constantly. At *C* the rhythm is decidedly irregular (similar to Ex. 55), but the chord-changes occur in the right place; therefore, while this does not remove the irregularity, it tends to clarify it.

A third method consists in prescribing an *sf* (*sforzando* accentuation) on any beat at option; if it stands on an unaccented beat, the rhythm is irregular. This is called the *dynamic* accentuation. Thus in the following (*A*, Beethoven, Op. 18, No. 5; *B*, Beethoven, Op. 18, No. 1):

At *A* the artificial accent is placed upon the unaccented second and fourth beats—a striking irregularity of which Beethoven made frequent use. (See also Ex. 60, D.) The rhythm at *B* is irregular both harmonically and dynamically. The student will find it to his advantage to observe rhythmic conditions in the music he is playing, and determine to which class belong the irregularities he will encounter—whether metric, harmonic or dynamic.

Cross-rhythms

The term, "cross rhythm," is generally applied to those complicated passages in which duple and triple meters occur simultaneously, in different parts of the harmony. The most common form is the cross rhythm of two notes against three, although many other combinations are effected. The following are outstanding examples (*A*, Schumann, Op. 22; *B*, Chopin, Op. 66; *C*, Chopin, Op. 32, No. 2; *D*, Brahms, Op. 79-1):

(A) The combination of two notes against three presents no difficulty to the performer, for the second note of the duplet falls exactly between the second and third notes of the triplet

and is therefore easily calculated. But the other mixtures are really difficult, because they cannot be thus calculated; in playing three notes against four (B) it is quite futile to measure off just where the uneven notes fall; the muscles must "swing" it, not the mind; one must merely keep the *beats* steady and regular. With three against five (C) or three against eight (D) this involuntary "swing" is still more imperative.

There are two specimens of cross rhythm which I am constrained to cite, since they assume peculiar significance (*A*, Schumann, Op. 12-1; *B*, Chopin, Op. 25-2):

Ex. 59

(A) Schumann was explicit enough; but he was so fearful of careless execution that he insisted, in a footnote, that the effect of 2-8 measure must predominate. To this end, a palpable accent should be given to the a-flat in the left hand, on the second beat; that is, the *left* hand marks the prescribed rhythm and should be made prominent. The case at (*B*) is similar, though the meters are reversed (triplet in the *left* hand). A certain writer who claimed that this is plainly a simple 6-4 measure, completely missed Chopin's intention; that would nullify one of the most ingenious and useful problems in the whole range of technical study. The only way to grasp the curious situation is to practice each hand separately for a while, giving marked emphasis to the four beat-notes of the *right* hand. See also the first theme of the slow movement of Brahms' "Piano Concerto in B flat"; the basic measure is 6-4, but the dominating melody is so suggestive of 3-2 that it is difficult to verify, by ear, the underlying rhythmic placing.

Dual Rhythms

Then there are the dual rhythms (perhaps the term, "mixed rhythms," would be more accurate). I refer to those fairly frequent cases in which, transiently, the effect of duple-meter is produced *within* a fundamental triple meter—or *vice versa*. For example, in the following (*A*, Beethoven, Op. 14, No. 2; *B*, Beethoven, "Symphony No. 4"; *C*, Beethoven, Op. 18, No. 6; *D*, Beethoven, "Symphony No. 3"; *E*, Schumann, "Concerto"):

At A, B, and D, the effect is plainly that of temporary duple meter, although the prevailing meter is triple. At C, the 3-4 measure assumes for quite a while the sound of 6-8. E, the passage from Schumann's "Concerto" (*Finale*) is famous for its persistence—page after page is clearly duple (within triple meter) —and for its pitfalls; I have known more than one distinguished virtuoso to come to grief and lose contact with the orchestra in this splendidly effective but insidious episode.

Other Unusual Rhythms

Another unusual rhythmic transformation is the "shifted measure." That is, a melodic sentence is sometimes shifted, usually forward, to a different place in the measure, whereby the rhythmic arrangement is completely altered. For example, in Bach's "Well-tempered Clavichord":

Ex.61 Original location: Shifted:

Lack of space contravenes my desire to give you more illustrations of these significant rhythmic conditions. Play your pieces more searchingly than hitherto and you will encounter examples aplenty.

In very rare instances the original differentiated form of a sentence is "ironed out," so to speak, so that the animated countenance of the theme assumes a sort of idiotic blankness, interesting in its way. Such equalized rhythm, for instance, appears in Ignace Friedman's "Passacaglia."

Ex.62 Original form:

Equalized:

This is a curious retrograde process, reversing that of evolution by reducing a developed product to its original, primitive elements; but it is a noteworthy test of the resources of rhythm.

Imbroglio is a term generally applied to any uneven mix-up of rhythmic figures. Here again, one specimen must suffice, although this is a fairly frequent device—Beethoven's "Symphony No. 8."

Ex.63

This is comparatively regular, in its constant shifting, resembling Ex. 60. But often the imbroglio is more complex and intentionally confusing.

Of that rare disruptive process, "dislocated" or "distorted" rhythm, the most striking example occurs in the second movement of Beethoven's "Symphony No. 3," *Funeral March on the Death of a Hero.* It seems inconsistent with the disposition of this titanic champion of absolute music, that he, Beethoven, should have deliberately adopted a "program" for this movement; and yet it requires no stretch of fancy to recognize therein a tone-picture of the successive episodes in the career of a hero, closing with his death. The first sentence is a sort of martial hymn:

which the dying hero chants at the end, in the following broken utterance. Not a tone is altered—only the rhythm:

The other orchestral instruments mark the fundamental rhythm and thus set forth the incoherent form. A parallel case, though simpler, may be seen in the final phrases of Beethoven's Overture to "Coriolanus."

Irregular Measures

Regarding unusual measure groups, the most common one is 5-4, which is purely the *combination* of duple and triple meters. It is (or should be) always either 2+3, with accents on the first and third beats, or 3+2, accented on the first and fourth beats. In the former (2+3) the *third* accent comes a beat later than is expected, for we are naturally prone to "count" regularly "2+2," and we look for an accent after the fourth beat. This imparts to 2+3 measure a hesitating, dragging effect, which has its charm, and presents no difficulty if maintained strictly throughout the phrase, or piece. The other form, 3+2, has the opposite effect: the third accent comes a beat sooner than expected, and the measure seems to stumble forward. The former combination is far the most common; its leisurely, swinging effect is the chief charm of the following famous example, from Tchaikovsky's "Pathetic Symphony":

An example of 5-4 measure, strictly 2+3, with a *dotted* bar line after the second beat, occurs in the "Symphony in B flat" of d'Indy, last movement. Another example appears in Op. 19 of Tchaikovsky; this latter, and the slow movement of Chopin's "Sonata, Op. 5," is wanting in a definite placing of the accents, so that one must contrive to hold *all five* beats together, which is disconcerting.

There is a fine example of 7-4 measure in the "Dante Symphony" of Liszt. It is lengthy and strictly 3+4. In the same work a passage in 5-4 occurs.

Not a single example of 5-4 have I found in Bach, Haydn, Mozart, Beethoven, Schubert, Schumann or Mendelssohn. An example of 3+2+2 occurs in the "Trio in C minor" of Brahms.

The Ragged Rhythm

Syncopation, the result of *tying* a weak unit of the measure to the stronger one, is so common and well understood that further comment here is needless. See the 33rd "Song Without Words," left hand; also Nos. 14, and 47.

It is needless to point out the very marked variations in the effects of melodies, made possible by the manifold rhythmic irregularities shown in the foregoing. They resemble the shifting punctuations in the famous muddle of Quince, as *Prologue*, in *Scene 1, Act 5,* of "Midsummer-Night's Dream." Or, the inviting sign in a barber's shop: *What do you | think—I'll | shave you for | nothing and | give you a | drink!* Challenged by a customer who refused to pay, the barber recited his sign thus: *What!— | —do you think I'll | shave you for | nothing and | give you a | drink?*

The altered meaning involved in this shifting of the punctuation marks is, in *literary* examples, certain to be humorous. But, humor in *music,* while doubtless possible and genuine enough, is so vague, and even visionary, that our similar rhythmic metamorphoses are often serious, legitimate and extremely important.

SELF-TEST QUESTIONS

1. What important function of music does rhythm represent?
2. In what respect is music totally unlike the arts of painting, sculpture, and architecture?
3. Which of the arts, on the contrary, is most similar to music?
4. How does rhythm vitalize music?
5. Name the successive divisions of time, which furnish the basis for all rhythmic distinctions.
6. How many kinds of "meter" are there; how named; and how distinguished?
7. What is the natural accent? What is "accentuation"?
8. When is the rhythm "regular," and when "irregular"?
9. Name the three kinds of artificial accentuation.
10. What are "cross-rhythms"?
11. What are "dual" or mixed rhythms?
12. What is the "shifted measure"; the "equalized rhythm"; the Imbroglio; the "dislocated" rhythm?
13. Explain 5-4 measure.
14. What is syncopation?

CHAPTER 8

WHY, AND HOW, WE USE NEIGHBORING NOTES

It is an interesting and extremely significant fact pertaining to our theoretical system of tone association that the separate tones do not always present themselves as *single* units, completely rounded out and limited exclusively to their resonant boundaries in the scale or chord, but that every one of them is surrounded by four neighbors with which it communicates, back and forth, chiefly, if not wholly, as a means of embellishment. It is as if each tone, while preserving its identity and its essential quality as definite pitch-entity, represents also a round group of five tones which share with each other in the established harmonic and melodic functions of the central tone. Glance at Ex. 68.

The central tone is called, of course, the principal or essential tone; the other four, which describe a sort of halo around it, are relatively unessential and may be used or not, at will, in coöperation with the chief unit. These unessential tones have been differently named (auxiliary, embellishing, foreign, inharmonic tones), but I have always felt that the most appropriate and lucid term for them is *neighboring* tones. For they lie invariably *next* above and below the principal tone, either at the distance of a whole-step or a half-step, according to conditions that will be disclosed as we proceed with their examination: two above, and two below, as contiguous whole or half steps. Thus, the tone G, for example, no matter what its location and its harmonic and melodic significance may be, is surrounded by A-flat and A, above, and F-sharp and F, below. These are the four neighbors of G; and unless they should prove to be principal tones themselves (by the movements and exigencies of the chords), they serve no higher purpose than to ornament their central tone.

But remember that the Neighbor is always the next higher or lower *letter*—never the same letter (as chromatic inflection). The upper neighbor of C is db—*not* c♯. Of Ab, the upper neighbors are bb and bbb.

Here is the tone G, for instance, and its four neighbors:

The neighboring notes will be indicated everywhere by the cypher (o) ; it is the most appropriate symbol, for the neighbors are zero quantities; they have no harmonic value whatever and only subserve the melodic lines in the capacity of embellishments.

In this example we have the tone G with its four neighbors, which huddle about their principal tone like chicks around a hen. The second measure is a random illustration of the manner in which the neighbors pass to and fro about their essential tone.

Location of the Neighboring Notes

There is, naturally, a choice between the whole-step and half-step neighbors, above and below. And this choice is determined as follows: the *upper* neighbor always agrees with the scale of the momentary key—somewhat rarely as lowered 6th or 2nd steps; the *lower* neighbor may also (and usually does) agree with the scale, but is rather frequently the half-step, as raised scale-step. Thus, in the key of C:

In the first measure, the upper neighbor is a whole step and the lower one a half step from the principal tone, both being common to the scale in question (C major). In the second measure each neighbor lies a whole step distant; in the third measure they are respectively a half step above and a whole step below. In measure 5, the lower neighbor is the half step, F-sharp; this is preferable to the scale-tone, F, because the latter, as 4th step, has a strong inclination to descend to E (as demonstrated in our sixth chapter) which is counteracted by raising (altering) it to F-sharp. Listen to it. The reason for preferring G-sharp, in the sixth measure, is quite different, but scarcely less cogent; play this measure (and *listen*) first with G-natural and then with G-sharp, and you will surely sense the harmonic condition involved, which makes G-sharp sound far more melodious and smooth than G-natural. In the 7th measure, the lower neighbor (A) will, however, not be altered to A-sharp, simply because the latter would be the raised 6th scale-step, which, as we have learned, is a rare alteration. The ear, if to any extent musically susceptible or trained, is the most reliable guide in determining the location of the lower neighbor; the *upper* one, as already stated, is free from all doubt, being always the next higher scale-step.

Consequently, if the C that occurs at the beginning of Ex. 68 (as keynote of C) happens to be the C in B-flat major, or in A-flat major, its neighbors will be different ones from those there seen. Thus:

At A both neighbors are a whole step from the principal tone; at B the upper one is a half step and the lower one a whole step; at C each neighbor is a half step distant (b-natural is here again the raised 4th step).

How They Enter

One might expect that the principal tone would be obliged to precede its neighboring notes; or, in other words, that a neighboring note may not appear until the principal tone has been sounded. This is not the case; the neighbors are not obliged thus to follow their principal tone, but may leap into being, free, abrupt, as if simply set before the latter—as if the voice aimed for the principal tone but struck its upper or lower edge. A neighbor which stands thus at the very beginning of a melodic figure, preceding its principal tone, is the form of melodic embellishment known as the appoggiatura (or, if very short, the acciaccatura); it may enter upon the scene from any angle and is often most unexpected, though never unwelcome if it subsequently behaves itself; its only obligation to its principal tone is that it *must* be absorbed by the latter—as we shall presently see. For illustration:

(A) Haydn's "Military Symphony," and (B) Mozart's "Alla Turca":

Ex. 70

At A the entire melodic sentence begins with a neighboring note, A, the upper neighbor of the keynote, G. It leaps into existence from "nowhere," relying solely upon its relation, as embellishment, to its principal tone, which promptly absorbs it. Precisely the same conditions obtain at B; the very first note of the piece is an upper neighbor of the keynote A. This B, at the beginning of the third full measure, is taken with a flying leap from the preceding E. See also Ex. 74, C, second and fourth beats. One of the most ingenious and poetically significant examples of the free entrance of the neighboring note is the following, from Op. 82, No. 7, of Schumann (*Vogel als Prophet*):

Ex. 71

The chords are plainly indicated by the groups of three thirty-second notes. The effect of these "free" neighboring notes is greatly heightened by their unusual length and weight—they usurp very nearly the whole beat. If you will take the trouble to consult (and play) the original, you will gain at once a full understanding of the significant function that may be assigned to the appoggiatura.

How They Progress

So much for the manner in which a neighbor may enter— either following its principal tone like a docile child (Ex. 68), or leaping into being (Exs. 70, 71). As to the manner in which it is disposed of, the following is to be considered: one of the most rigorous rules in the entire system of tone obligation is that the neighboring tone should fall back into its principal tone. This is known as its "resolution" and is so rational and consistent that it calls for no justification or apology. Still, we might illustrate it with, say, a bean and a bowl: if we drop the bean exactly into the center of the bowl, it will stay where it falls; for the center is analogous to the principal tone, which, being a part of the chord, requires no further guaranty of its stability. But if we hold our hand an inch or so to the left or right and drop the bean so that it strikes the inside edge of the bowl (Ex. 70), the bean must invariably roll down until it reaches the center of the bowl, the resting place. Hence the rule that the neighbor must resolve into its principal tone.

The Passing Notes

But the rule works out in two or three other ways that are unexpected though quite as legitimate and natural as the normal resolutions. The first of these is the case in which the neighboring note shifts its responsibility from one principal tone to another. The "halos" or rings of neighbors overlap, so that the same neighbor belongs to two different principal tones. Thus, in the chord of C (c-e-g), the note *d* is the upper neighbor of C and, at the same time, the lower neighbor of E. Therefore, while it may enter from C, it is free to exercise its allegiance *in either direction;* it may return to C, or it may *pass on* over into E. In the latter case it becomes a *passing note,* and as such is almost more common than the simple neighboring note, for it possesses the two advantages of forward movement and of smoothness. In the following (A, Beethoven, Op. 10, No. 2; B, Op. 2, No. 2), the passing notes are marked "x" for distinction:

The B-flat at the end of the first measure is the upper neighbor of the chord tone, A-flat, and, at the same time, the lower neighbor of C. It simply transfers its obligation from one to the other and becomes a connecting link between the two principal tones. When the space between the chord-tones is wider than a third, two passing notes may be inserted, as in the second measure at B; the first neighbor (F-sharp) is the lower neighbor of the next neighbor (G-sharp, lower neighbor of the chord-tone A); thus they help each other out, basing their connection upon the continuity inherent in the scale. In fact, when chromatic, three or even four passing notes may occur in succession, usually in swift tempo. For example, Beethoven, Op. 2, No. 2:

The second of these exceptional cases occurs when one neighbor leaps a third over into the other neighbor, of the same principal tone, the latter following immediately and resolving them both. It most commonly happens that the lower neighbor leaps upward into the upper one, although the opposite is possible. The following examples are A, from Schubert, Op. 78; B, Mozart, "Sonata in F"; and C, Verdi, "Aida":

At A, the lower neighbor (C-sharp) leaps over into the upper one (E), and their common principal tone follows and absorbs them both. At B, the upper neighbor (E-flat) comes first, and then the lower one (C-sharp, raised second scale-step). See also the first two measures in the second movement of Beethoven's 8th Symphony; and the famous E-flat *Rondo* of Weber.

In some rare instances the second one of the neighbors leaps back again into the first one, before the principal tone appears, in which case we have a triple-neighbor; and even similar quadruple neighbors are possible, though extremely uncommon. Thus in Beethoven, Op. 110; in Chopin, Op. 61; and in the "Flower Dance" of Tchaikovsky we have:

Older writers contented themselves with one neighbor at a time; one encounters the double-neighbor very rarely in music prior to Bach or Scarlatti; the triple-neighbor seems to have waited for Beethoven's all-encompassing vision, and the quadruple-neighbor cited in the foregoing, appears to owe its inception to Chopin. It is becoming a little more popular with modern writers; there is an example of Debussy's in which the two neighbors bob back and forth like rubber balls a dozen times before their principal tone puts a stop to the silly game. One is impelled to question apprehensively, "What next?"

The third of our exceptional cases, the unresolved neighbor, is decidedly wilful, emancipated; but it cannot be regarded as wholly lawless, since it is sanctioned by Mozart and all classic masters, and is more common than might be expected: I mean the case in which one neighbor (almost always the *upper* one) leaps a third, usually quickly, into another neighbor—as it has a right to do—but does not *return* to its principal tone for resolution. This phenomenon can be made plainer with notes than with words (A, Beethoven, Op. 2, No. 3; B, Mozart, *Sonata in A*):

Ex.76

At A, the upper neighbor (A) leaps down a third to the lower one (F-sharp), and that is the end of it; the common principal tone, G-sharp, does not follow. The same conditions prevail in the next measure. Both of these "free" neighbors are fully justified, theoretically, by the fact that they are "absorbed" by the following *chord,* to which they harmonically may belong, and are known as "anticipations." But even this argument fails in the Mozart example (B), for the upper neighbors, first the D and then the F-sharp, are not thus "absorbed." Their chief excuse is their brevity; the whole ornament passes so quickly that one does not realize what has happened, and need not care.

One other not unusual irregularity may be recorded, and that is the neighbor-of-the-neighbor. For example, notice this passage from Chopin, Op. 59, No. 3:

Ex.77

The D at the beginning of the second measure is the upper neighbor of the chord tone C-sharp; it is embellished with *its* upper neighbor, E, which is also foreign to the chord. It is a favorite figure of Chopin's. One is reminded of Dean Swift's whimsical epigram:

> ——*a flea*
> *Has smaller fleas that on him prey,*
> *And these have smaller still to bite 'em——*

All of these neighboring notes are generally very brief, as has been seen. They pass quickly, serving merely to embellish, with a quick movement, some essential tone or tones. It is precisely because of the uncommon length and emphasis of the neighboring notes in Ex. 71 that Schumann has achieved so striking and original an effect.

The Organ Point

To this there is, however, one important exception, and that is the so-called organ-point. This is a long tone, often very long, held (generally in the bass voice) in obstinate disregard of the chord movements in the upper parts. From time to time, as these chords change, the sustained tone in the bass becomes inharmonic (foreign). At such moments it is a "neighboring note," of course, for every tone that is not in the chord must be a neighbor of some tone that is a chord interval. One example (Brahms, "Symphony No. 3") of the organ-point must suffice here:

Ex. 78
Andante

The C in the bass is a brief organ point (during the second beat). Get this right: it is not the fact that the bass tone is *held* that makes it an organ-point, for very often the bass is sustained through long repetitions of the chord, or related chords, but the fact that at some point it becomes foreign to the chord—as on the second beat in this example. See also Beethoven, Op. 28, the first twenty measures; the throbbing D in the bass is a long organ point. See also Ex. 80, D.

The Ornaments

Of the most common melodic ornaments, the most important, if not the oldest, is probably the trill. But the following list includes all those in common use—not nearly as freely now, however, as in the olden days of profuse melodic ornamentation:

Ex. 79

a. Trill (1. classic manner; 2. modern method)
b. Inverted trill (Beethoven. Op. 27, No. 1.)
c. Mordent
d. Inverted mordent
e. Turn
f. Inverted turn
g. Appoggiatura
h. Acciaccatura

a.   The trill, in its original form, and throughout the classic era, always *began with the upper neighbor;* nowadays, the ruling notion is that it should begin with the principal tone. It would be well for the player to bear this in mind; and, in any case, the classic method almost always simplifies the rhythm of the "final turn" (with the opposite neighbor) with which the trill generally terminates.

b.   For the inverted trill (the principal tone alternating with its *lower* neighbor) there is no sign; it must always be written out, as shown in our example.

c.   The mordent on a principal tone alternates with its *lower* neighbor; "d" is the reverse.

e.   A turn always begins with the upper neighbor; and, as shown, the turn may be placed upon the chief tone, or *between* it and the next.

f.   The inverted turn is rare, usually not indicated by the turn-sign upside down, but written out.

g and h. The difference between these is solely that one is quicker than the other. They occupy the accent.

Unusual Tone-combinations

The varieties of peculiar, freakish, often perplexing "combinations" that result from ingenious (or reckless) use of neighboring notes are almost innumerable; they constitute one of the chief resources of unexpectedly lovely and always interesting effects—when the composer is sensitive (and sensible) enough to guard the limits of endurable dissonance and so to handle the tones (by early "resolution") as to make the underlying harmonic identity perfectly clear. I cannot refrain from exhibiting a few of these, gleaned at random from classic works. The curious complex tone-bodies are marked with an asterisk:

a. Brahms, Op. 116, No. 6 (simplified)
b. Chopin, Op. 59, No. 1
c. Wagner, "Der Ring des Nibelungen"
d. Mendelssohn, Op. 82
e. Beethoven, Op. 2, No. 1
f. Beethoven, Op. 22

A most extraordinary example of four neighbors at once appears at C. Each one is a half-step from its principal tone; this is singularly beautiful, when one has grasped the whole harmonic situation, as one inevitably will upon a third or fourth patient hearing. The whole is justified by the baleful, tragic dramatic context, and is scientifically faultless, as perhaps only a genius can manage such hazardous effects. Note the simultaneous F-flat and F-sharp (6th step raised and lowered at the same moment), and the unusual length of the neighbors. At D there is a rare instance of all seven tones of the scale together at once; C-sharp and E-natural are the raised fourth and sixth steps; D in the bass is an organ-point. The chord is the altered IV_7, of G minor.

The young player jumped up from the piano exclaiming, "Oh, Mama! I found a misprint in Beethoven's very first sonata!" What seems to support *her* error is the fact that the D-flat and D-natural appear together quite alone (see E).

I saved the best for the last illustration: (F) the tone-cluster in the first measure (right hand) *looks,* on the keyboard, like the dominant-seventh chord of G-flat, and would sound like it, if played alone, with D-flat and C-flat, instead of C-sharp and B-natural; and the one in the second measure *looks,* if detached, like the dominant-seventh of A (with G-sharp in place of A-flat).

A neighbor entering as repetition, like the B-natural on the accent, in Ex. 80, A, is known as a "suspension"—the same with A in the next measure. Call it what you like, it is a neighboring note.

These fascinating specimens of unique tone-grouping might be multiplied indefinitely, but space forbids. All such perplexing tone-combinations are unintelligible when isolated; they must be judged with their surroundings—that is, with what *follows* them; for the true master, fully aware of the scientific conditions involved, always resolves each foreign tone promptly and properly. Therefore the student must learn to look ahead; for it is what a tone *does,* that must establish its identity. I trust this essay will stimulate you to take your practice more seriously and to peer beneath the surface of the notes, at least to distinguish between the tones that are a part of the chord, and those that are only ornamental neighbors.

There is an alluring hypothesis involved in this comprehensive principle of neighboring notes that has haunted me all my life, one to which I have never before given expression. This seems the most appropriate moment for its elucidation. It is this: that the dominant and second-dominant (subdominant) harmonies are, in point of location, and perhaps from deeper causes, merely the *neighbors of the tonic chord*. If this be accepted, then the trinity of chords which we have shown to be the three life-roots of the entire harmonic growth (tonic, dominant and subdominant) is reduced to one central element, the tonic, to which every tone in music can be referred. This seems rational, and there are proofs enough of this conception in classic music. For illustration, see the following from Schubert, Op. 78 (A); and Beethoven, "Symphony No. 3" (B):

It is chiefly, of course, a question of the *length* of the "neighboring chords"; the mind must have time to grasp the full harmonic quality of a chord, as such; and surely the groups of sixteenth notes at A are far too transient for this purpose, and the same is true of the apparent IV at B, alternating like a double trill with the consonant tonic chord. These are all neighboring chords. See also Beethoven, 7th Symphony, 3rd movement, *presto meno assai;* the chords in eighth-notes are too brief to be essential (measures 1 to 4; 9 to 12). Also see Beethoven, "Sonata Op. 2, No. 3," last movement; the rapid "chords" are passing groups.

Be all this as it may, the fact remains that all but one tone of the dominant-ninth chord are neighbors of the tonic; and similarly, nearly all the tones of the second-dominant chords are neighbors of the tonic—whether or not they are long enough to produce an independent harmonic impression.

SELF-TEST QUESTIONS

1. How many "neighboring notes" belong to each essential tone, and where are they located?
2. Which are the four neighbors of A?
3. How is their notation defined?
4. How do they enter; how do they progress?
5. How is the passing note formed?
6. What leap from a neighbor is allowed?
7. Define the organ-point?
8. Define each of the principal ornaments—trill, mordent, turn, appoggiatura.
9. What is the old rule of playing the trill?
10. What reasonable limits are imposed upon the formation of unusual tone-combinations?
11. In which composition are all seven tones of the scale presented together?
12. Where do you find an example of four simultaneous neighbors?

CHAPTER 9

How, and Why, Keys Intermingle—Modulation

We have learned to regard the key as a Family of tones. The term "Tonality" is applied to a broader concept and signifies the whole community of more or less closely related tone-families or keys, which interact and associate on the same principles as those that control the intermingling of the chords themselves within a key, only on a larger scale.

The conception of tonality is usually limited to those half-dozen keys that are closely related to each other; but, in its wider sense, tonality concerns the large community which embraces every key in common use in music, all so interwoven and inter-related that it is possible to connect any two keys in the whole range of the tone-universe. When we start on a journey we may go on and on until we circle the globe; and we may encounter friends or acquaintances in the most remote countries. To be sure, there are natural limits; one is more likely to associate inti-mately and frequently with near-by neighbors than with relatives in distant cities; and, accordingly, while C major *may* make contact with G-sharp major or E-flat minor (compare Ex. 90), such remote contacts will be more rare and brief than the alternation of C major with, say, G major or A minor.

These exchanges of key—the passing from one over into another—are called modulations.

Key-Relationships

The first step in the investigation of the necessity, causes and processes of modulation consists in defining the degree of relation between the keys; and for this we need, first of all, to review the diagram of key-formation given in Ex. 3 (first chapter). For the basis of tone-relationship is as broad as it is immutable, and ap-plies to every dimension in music. Ex. 82 may be referred to for an illustration of this broad principle.

Any two keys are distinguished either as *next related, re-motely related,* or *foreign* (comparatively non-related) to each other; and these distinctions are defined, at least primarily, simply according to the number of scale-tones which are common to the two keys. A comparison of the scales of C and G major, for example, discloses only one differentiated tone: F-natural in C becomes F-sharp in G; all the rest of the tones are alike in both keys. Therefore, these two keys are next-related, and intercourse between them is easy.

There is, however, an easier and really more conclusive way of fixing key-relations, and that is, naturally, by applying the basic law of tone-relations as revealed in the fundamental chart of the *chords* within a key. Thus, in the key of C:

Ex. 82

It goes without saying that each of these triads (excepting the VII) may be the tonic chord of a key; and the keys thus represented are, unquestionably, related to each other in precisely the same manner and degree as are the chords which constitute the single family. Thus the IV indicates the tonic chord of F major; the V is the index of G major; the II of D minor; the VI, A minor; and the III, E minor. The VII (or incomplete dominant-seventh) indicates no key, since it has no perfect fifth and hence no dominant of its own.

The scales of these keys differ from the scale of C at only one point (only excepting D minor and E minor, which, in their harmonic form, differ at two points); consequently the next-related keys of C major are F and G major, D, A and E minor.

Central key	Next-related keys
C major	F major
	G major
	D minor
	A minor
	E minor

In other words, each major and minor triad may become the tonic center of a key, and the selfsame degree and quality of relation exists between these several keys as obtains between the chords themselves.

But there is still another, even more simple and direct, method of determining the degree of relation or non-relation between keys, and that is the comparison of their *signatures*. For the signature of a key is literally what it claims to be—a "signature," an exact index of the contents. The signatures are the milestones on the musical turn-pike, the sharps running, say, north, and the flats, south. Or more correctly, they are the numbers of the floors in our music-apartment, lying above and below the central one.

Since C major has been adopted as the central key with no signature (or the zero signature) it is clear that the signature of, for example, three sharps, indicates that there are three tones in its scale which differ from the tones of the C major scale; hence, A major is three degrees removed from C major in the community of keys. C major takes its place in the center, or on level ground; the sharp-signatures accumulate in perfect fifths *upward* from C, the flat-signatures similarly *downward;* therefore we say that A major lies three degrees above C major—A-flat four degrees *below* C, and so on. These points in the endless chain of perfect fifths (see the last example in our first chapter) are fixed for the major keys, primarily; but it must not be forgotten that (as shown in the fifth chapter) every signature serves for two keys, a minor as well as a major, and these both confirm the degree of key-relationship in exactly the same manner, irrespective of the "number of common tones." Thus, F-sharp minor (with the three-sharp signature) stands in the same relation to C major as does A major.

It must be emphasized, in passing, that the purposes, operations and effects of the entire modulatory system consist in nothing more evident and significant than these journeys *upward* and *downward* through the tone-realm. Modulation converts the level plain into a panorama of hills and valleys; one feels the upward tension, the downward relaxation, the "ups and downs" (a sort of musical scenic railway) which break the monotony of life, dramatize, vitalize and fill it with the realities of checkered existence. Therefore we speak of modulating from C *up* to G or D, and *down* from C to F or E-flat, and so forth. (The modulation from any key to another one that has the same signature, say C major to A minor, is a momentary *level* stretch that is just as welcome and essential as ascent and descent.)

To summarize: (1) We thus define the five next-related keys as being like the next-door neighbors of the central one, with which we can therefore exchange visits, brief or prolonged, conveniently and as frequently as we like.   (2) These next-related keys are defined by simply comparing the signatures—bearing in mind that those with sharps lie above and those with flats lie below the central one.   (3) There are always two keys with the same signature whose relations to the others are exactly the same, in all modulatory excursions.

When and How Keys Change

Modulation—which is ecstasy to the master but something of a puzzle and bugbear to the beginner—is an extremely simple matter, and the student who faces the problem fearlessly and from the proper angle need not fear.

There are numberless ways of changing a key, some clumsy, and others skillful and refined; and various theorists have suggested specific methods and defended them as the easiest and best; they are often ingenious and usually valid. Perhaps the most widely circulated theory is that one should make the modulation through some chord that is *common to both keys concerned.* This is theoretically unassailable, but it involves a harmonic calculation which cannot always be quickly made, especially in improvisation, and it is totally refuted in the domain of chromatics. Let me illustrate this method with a passage from Beethoven, Op. 14, No. 1:

Ex. 83

The first chord in the third measure is still in G, as the triad VII; at the same time it may be (and in this case is) the II of E minor; it is common ground, and may be used in either of its two identities; asserting itself as II, it changes the key from G to E. If we should substitute D-natural for the D-sharp in the bass, the key would remain G. The D-sharp turns the current.

The Fundamental Rule

But the best rule I have ever found, and one that is employed in the very great majority of cases, is this: lead the harmony to any *tonic concord,* in any form; from there, any change of key is easy. The reasons for this are clear: the tonic harmonies are points of conclusion and rest; they consummate all pending "resolutions," leave nothing unfinished and therefore rather invite change than antagonize it; no landlord can object to your moving out if you have paid your rent and put your house in order. When you strike a tonic chord you "touch bottom" and are free to move

in *any* direction.   And it must be remembered that, as shown in
our third chapter, there are *two* tonic chords, the triads I and VI,
either one of which serves the purpose.   For example, in Beethoven, Op. 14, No. 2.

Ex. 84 Andante

The first beat of the second measure rounds out the C major
motive almost as completely as if it were the end of the piece; and
so it is perfectly easy to "switch off" at that tonic point, into a
new key.   The same conditions obtain in each of the modulations
in the second fragment.

These illustrations are taken from the Andante movement
of Beethoven's *Sonata, Op. 14, No. 2;* and it is noteworthy that
every one of the five next-related keys (of the original C major)
is represented in the whole theme, namely: A minor, G major (3
times), F, D minor (3 times) and E minor—these and no others.

But there is a very important second clause to our rule.   It
is one thing to get *out* of a key, and easy enough with the above
rule; but it is quite a different matter to pass smoothly *into* the
key one aims for.   Hence this addition to the rule: enter the new
key, as a rule, with any one of its *dominant* chords; for these
contain the leading-tone (7th step) whose main function it is to
proceed into and confirm the keynote.   This is precisely what
happens in every case, in Ex. 84, and in fact throughout the Andante theme.   Furthermore, this will be found to be the chosen
method nine times out of ten, in the music of the classic masters.
For this reason we shall call this the *fundamental* rule of modulation.

Other Methods

Still, there are other ways of doing it; one may also enter the new key through any of its subdominant (second-dominant) chords—the IV, II, II$_7$—because these lead normally into the decisive dominant. Thus, from Mendelssohn's *Wedding March:*

Ex. 85

Here each key, first C, then E minor, end on their tonic chords; the new keys, E minor and the final C major, both begin with one of their second-dominant chords.

These are the chords which possess the needed driving power; but the other one of the three principal chord-families, the tonic class itself, is, fundamentally, powerless to carry us into a new key. It can be done, when circumstances are propitious and when a master hand guides it; but the novice should not attempt to enter a new key through the tonic of that key, on the principle that you cannot board a car if you are already in it. And yet there *is* one very important exception to this apparently self-evident rule: one *can* enter a new key with one particular form of the tonic, and that is the 6-4 form, *on an accent*—for the accented I$_2$ tends almost irresistibly to reach the dominant, and so we get the proper chord after all. See the beats marked * in the following, from Beethoven, Op. 14, No. 2:

Ex. 86

The "2" at the right of the numeral "I" signifies "second inversion"—fifth of the chord in the bass.

Our fundamental rule then reads thus: "Close the old key upon some form of its tonic harmony, and enter the desired key through any form of its dominant, or second- (sub-) dominant chords; or, more rarely, with the accented tonic 6-4 chord.

Chromatic Modulation

A melodic progression is diatonic when it follows the line of the scale from letter to letter. The chromatic progression, on the other hand, consists in the inflection of a letter by means of an accidental (sharp, flat, natural, double sharp or double flat). The diatonic movements are natural, the chromatic ones artificial; and the distinction is very marked. The chromatic succession is always somewhat forced and abrupt, though not rude, and everywhere possible. Diatonics run obediently in the path of the scale; chromatics make a sidewise twist, in defiance of the scale.

A modulation is chromatic when one or more of the voices are thus deflected in passing from the last chord of the old key into the first one of the new. The last measure in Ex. 84 contains a chromatic modulation from F to D minor, since it involves C to C-sharp in the left hand (see also the first measure in Ex. 86; also Ex. 89).

A curious trait of chromatics is that they may set aside our fundamental rule. By making use of the chromatic inflection the change of key may be made from *any* chord. That is, it *may* be so; although in very many cases (as in Exs. 84 and 86) the transition, even when chromatic, does conform to the rule.

The following example is "exceptional" (Beethoven, Op. 2, No. 2):

Ex. 87

E minor   VII₇ G V₇

I   G VII₇ B♭V₇ I

The E minor ends on one of its dominant chords (third measure) which, theoretically, is the chord least likely to be chosen to finish a key with, since the dominant chords have such a strong natural tendency to lead into their tonic harmony; but the subtle force of the chromatic twist (d-sharp to d-natural, above) overcomes this tendency, without any disagreeable impression. The next case is similar: the last chord in G (7th measure) is a form of its dominant harmony—with an *altered step* (e-flat, the lowered 6th) that suggests the minor mode; the chromatic move from f-sharp to f-natural changes the key to B-flat major. Note that in both of these instances there are two different dominant discords *in succession,* which is another noteworthy concomitant of chromatics; such successions of dominant chords are often lengthy, usually smooth, but irrespective of key-relations. For example, from Beethoven, Op. 10, No. 3 (A); and a Chopin *Etude* (B):

Ex.88

A
D VII₇   C VII₇   G VII₇   D VII₇   I

B
Db V₇   D V₇   Eb V₇   E V₇   F V₇   Gb V₇   Db V₇

The chromatics are easy to locate.

It is in such progressions that the question arises, "How many chords or beats does it take to define a new key completely?" One may run over to a neighbor's place, stand and gossip a moment at the gate without entering the yard or house. What constitutes a full-fledged visit? The answer seems to depend on the individual; some musicians have so keen a tone-sense that they apprehend a full key-impression in a single beat, while others are so dull that they do not perceive actual key-changes that may occupy several beats. Some theorists declare that the first period in Mendelssohn's *Wedding March* (Ex. 85) is *all* in C major, and that the first phrases in Beethoven's "Symphony No. 1" all confirm, likewise, the key of C. I am sure this is erroneous; am convinced that both of these masters intended distinct modulations here. Now, to provide the student with a standard, I would suggest the following rule: a complete change of key cannot be *established* with less than two chords, and these must be the dominant and tonic harmonies in direct succession.   For instance, there appears in Beethoven, Op. 14, No. 2:

These are indisputably complete changes of key.

When, on the contrary, only *one* chord stands for its key, as in Ex. 88, I would call it a "passing" key, on exactly the principle that defines "passing" notes (see our eighth chapter).

With the altered chords the case is again different (see our fourth chapter); for an altered "chord" is not an altered "key." The distinction is a bit puzzling, but clear enough to an unblurred musical vision.   The list of altered steps is so accurately limited, and every altered chord is so hedged about with factors of the prevailing key (it usually enters from, and progresses into, the tonic chords) that no doubts need arise.   Still, every altered chord does "suggest" a different key, and, if you prefer, you may call it, too, a "passing" key.   However, there is not an iota of the characteristic essence of "alteration" in Ex. 88; each single chord is a passing key.

Remote Modulation

It is self-evident that modulations can be, and are, made most easily to and fro between the next-related keys, whose signatures being most nearly alike, are therefore *neighboring* keys.   But it may be desirable to make a call upon some more remote member of the tonality, and for this the composer often takes a bee-line. By adhering to the fundamental rule, and employing the effective agency of chromatics, any two keys, no matter how far apart, may be connected.   For example:

These fragments are exactly alike in effect; only the notation and the chromatic lines differ. They span in an instant the wide cleft between the key of C and those of six sharps or six flats.

Opposite Modes

But the most convenient and efficient means of reaching quickly a remote key consists in the readily practicable and extremely common interchange of modes. I mean what is known as the *Opposite modes of the same keynote*. It was shown, in our fifth chapter, that the major and minor modes of the same keynote are in all essential respects identical: C minor is nothing more than a modified (altered) form of C major; and since their signatures differ by three degrees (C major, natural scale; C minor, three flats) it follows that a single movement from one to the other covers this modulatory distance. Hence we encounter, very often, the direct change from C major to C minor (or *vice versa*) and between all similar "opposite modes"—as shown in the following example. A, from Schubert, Op. 78; B, Brahms' 3rd Symphony; C, Schubert, *Müllerlied:*

These illustrate the direct "change of mode." But there is another method of utilizing this coincidence between major and minor (of the same keynote) which is more comprehensive than the simple change of mode, and that is the *exchange* of mode. This consists in substituting minor for the *expected* major, or *vice versa*—expected because next-related. One aims for the next-related key (mode), but, like a person changing his mind while bent on an errand, substitutes the opposite mode at the last moment. For instance, the modulation from C major to A minor may become C major to A major, without altering the harmonic process; or C minor—G minor may become C minor—G major. This exchange is possible, with very few exceptions, and the underlying reason for it is as simple as it is significant—namely: the chords of the dominant family are alike (or may be made so) in both the major and minor mode of the same tonic. And it must be borne in mind that the dominant is the chord most frequently chosen for the entrance into a new key. Thus, in the key of C:

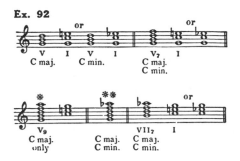

Ex. 92

* This is the one exception; the major form of the V⁹ is possible only in *major*.

** The A-flat, necessary for the minor mode, is, in major, the lowered sixth step—one of the most frequent of the altered steps. This can not be too strongly emphasized; the lowering of the sixth step is the first incident in the formation of the minor scale; and the subsequent lowering of the third step consummates the change. Hence, whenever the harmony touches a dominant chord (if a ninth, then with lowered sixth step), the composer is free to resolve it either into the major or minor tonic, absolutely at option; and thereupon rests the entire scheme of the exchange of mode. For illustration: A. From C to A (minor or major); B. C minor to G (minor or major); C. Beethoven, Op. 13; D. Beethoven, Op. 2, No. 3:

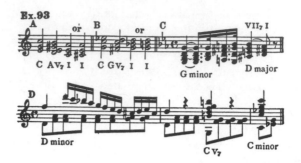

At A, after C major, one expects A minor, the next related key; by virtue of the ambiguous dominant, the remote A major may be substituted. The case at B is analogous. At C, the next-related key from G minor would be D minor; but D major is exchanged for it. At D, C minor is exchanged for the expected (because next-related) C major.

It is this exchange of mode that accounts for so many minor pieces ending in major; see nearly every minor fugue in Vol. I of Bach's "Well-tempered Clavichord"; also the last movement of Beethoven's symphonies Nos. 5 and 9, both of which are in minor, but end in the corresponding major.

Enharmonic Modulation

The direction of certain chords may be changed by substituting the "enharmonic equivalent" for one or more of its tones; that is, changing C-sharp to D-flat, G to F-double sharp, and the like. For example, the following from Beethoven, Op. 13:

Upon the repetition of the measure, the E-flat is altered enharmonically to D-sharp, and G minor is thereby deflected into E minor. See also Ex. 96, sixth measure.

Modulation at Cadences

It was shown, in the foregoing, that the best place to leave a key is at one of its tonic chords, since these are points of *conclu-*

sion. But this impression of having reached the end of a motive,
a corner, so to speak, where a change of direction may easily take
place, is most forcibly felt at any *cadence;* for a cadence is actually
the end of a melodic member. The cadence may be absolute,
marking the end of a whole section; or it may be a temporary
pause, or joint, between smaller members of the phrase—the point
where a singer takes a breath, or the player lifts his hand to define
the "phrasing"; the punctuation marks of the musical sentence.
At any such point it is easy to change the key, no matter what
chords are involved, and this is often done, abruptly, irrespective
of our fundamental rule, and sometimes with startling results.
For example: A, Chopin, Op. 24, No. 2; B, Mendelssohn, Op. 54;
C, Schubert, Op. 78.

The cadence in the second measure at A marks the complete ending of a large part. This is so final that *any* key can follow the
C major. Chopin has chosen D-flat major; it might about as well
have been D-major, E-flat major, and so forth. Try them all
yourself. B illustrates the fact that a Sequence is the restatement
of a figure upon other, higher or lower, steps. It automatically
punctuates the phrase, for there must be a "joint" where the
sequence begins. This example (B) defies the fundamental rule

in every respect.   Examples 83, 87, and 89 also illustrate *sequence* modulation.

I cannot conclude the story of key-intercourse without citing a remarkable example of the uncanny skill of Schubert (Op. 90, No. 3), who was the wizard of modulation:

In the brief limits of a single phrase, he passes from G (one sharp) to A-flat minor (seven flats) and quickly back, utilizing the exchange of mode and an enharmonic change: the C-sharp and A-sharp are the raised fourth and second steps of G major.

Historians say that Schubert never studied; they mean that he gave scant attention to textbooks.   He went straight to headquarters and studied the music of the masters, with a keenness that is rarely equalled.   You also may need no textbooks if you will follow Schubert's example.   Still, good textbooks do *facilitate* study.

SELF-TEST QUESTIONS

1. What is modulation?
2. Name the three degrees of relationship between keys.
3. How is key-relation most readily determined?   (Name the process which defines next-relation, and the simple comparison which fixes every degree of relation.)
4. What theory of key-change has been widely adopted?
5. Define the fundamental rule of modulation.
6. Does the chromatic progression sometimes nullify this rule?
7. How many chords are necessary to establish a key?

8. When is a modulation remote, and how can it be easily made?
9. What is meant by the opposite modes?
10. Which is the only dominant chord that is *not* common to both major and minor?
11. Why can a modulation be easily effected at any cadence, or joint?

CHAPTER 10

The Most Wonderful Chord in Music

Many of my astute readers will guess at once, correctly, to which chord I refer; and they may "know all about it." But even these may discover in the following lines a few fascinating and valuable traits that have not chanced to come to their notice, not to speak of the great army of music lovers who may here make the intimate acquaintance of the most wonderful chord in music for the first time.

For the benefit of those who have not given much thought to it, or who may have preferences that run in a different direction, I would aver my unalterable conviction that the most wonderful chord in music is the *chord of the diminished seventh;* and the amazing, bewildering qualities that assure it this distinction are its great tonal beauty, its incredible flexibility, and its all-embracing capacity for emotional suggestion and expression. It can be passionate or demure, raging or gentle, exuberantly joyous or profoundly sorrowful, dramatic or pathetic—all depending upon its surroundings and the manner of its use. It is true, however, that its emotional effect is most frequently dramatic, fiery, often profoundly pathetic.

Since its most obvious trait, for the student, is its elusiveness, its apparent lack of any precise, definable quality, it is of the first importance to fix its *legitimate* location and name in the key.

But let me first reaffirm a statement made in one of the previous chapters, which, though not directly concerned in the consideration of the diminished-seventh chord, is so vital that it cannot be too emphatically reiterated.

The Family of Chords

There are some one hundred odd chords, counting all the various forms and inversions of the seven fundamental ones, in the major and minor modes (exclusive of the altered ones). And what must be impressed upon the student is the fact that all of these proceed out of *three basic roots,* the three principal triads: the tonic, the dominant, and the second-dominant (or supertonic, or subdominant, all of which designations are comprised under the title "second-dominant"). These three chords are the three life roots of the tonal tree; or, if you prefer, the three pillars of the music-edifice; there is not a single chord anywhere in genuine music, whether it appears in its plain form, or embellished with neighboring notes, that does not come under one or the other of these three heads. It *must* be either some form of the tonic harmony, or some form of the dominant body, or some form of the second-dominant harmony. This is inevitable, simply because there are no other sources of harmonic generation outside of these three.

It will not be amiss to tabulate them again here:

1. The *tonic* family consists of the I, the VI, and all of their inverted forms, also their sevenths and ninths.

2. The *dominant* family consists of the V, the V_7, V_9, VII, VII_7, and the III, with all their inversions.

3. The *second-dominant* family embraces the II, II_7, II_9, IV and IV_7, with all their inversions.

To this we might add:

1. The dominant family is characterized by the *presence* of the leading-tone (the seventh step of the key-scale).

2. The tonic and second-dominant bodies are both distinguished by the *absence* of the leading-tone; and they all contain the tonic (keynote).

3. In the tonic group this keynote is the root or third (consonant intervals); in the second-dominant class it is usually the seventh (dissonant interval).

4. In the dominant group, the leading-tone is the third of the chord, or the *apparent* root (in the incomplete forms).

And these chords all have the same names, locations and functions in minor as in major. Of them all, only the V, V_7, and VII have the same form in major and minor. The others all differ.

The Birthplace of the Diminished-Seventh Chord

Now, as to the diminished-seventh chord, upon which our attention is to be focused, it is such an ubiquitous imp, pervading the entire realm of harmony, assuming some different fanciful significance at every turn, that we must first pin it down to its one single responsible harmonic meaning, and, by defining its *original, legitimate* place in the key, secure a point of departure from which its antics can be observed and controlled.

First of all, the diminished-seventh chord is an offspring of the *minor mode*. Further, it belongs, legitimately, to the *dominant* family; wherefore, it contains the leading-tone. And, finally, its proper place in the key is indicated by its original name, the VII_7. It is, therefore, the chord of the seventh upon the seventh step of the minor mode, or, the incomplete form of the dominant-ninth chord (that is, the V_9 with its root omitted); its *apparent* root—the tone upon which it is erected in superposed thirds—is the seventh step, or leading-tone, of the minor mode.

All of these details are necessary for its definition, because they all converge to determine its one single *legitimate* location and its movements. For illustration, in the key of C, minor mode:

Ex. 97   also:

Tonic   Dom.   V V_7 V_9 VII_7 C minor   C major

The distinctive item in its name, "diminished seventh," is derived from the fact that the uppermost tone of the structure of thirds (the seventh of the chord) is a *diminished* interval—b♮, a♭. Review, if you like, our second and third chapters.

Our diminished-seventh chord, then, is the VII_7, the dominant ninth with omitted root—the chord of the seventh on the leading-tone of the minor mode. The last measures of Ex. 97 disclose the first evidence of the ambiguity of the chord; although its original dwelling place is *minor,* it is quite as much at home in major, though in that case its seventh (here a♭) must be accounted for as the lowered sixth step. The exact agreement of the dominant family in major and minor (with but one single exception), made possible by the lowering of the sixth step, was shown in Ex. 92 of our preceding chapter.

Now we must resort to the keyboard in order to discover the first cause of the perplexing ambiguity of the diminished-seventh chord. It consists of four practically (not actually) equal divisions of the full chromatic octave, each higher tone being the interval of *three half-steps* from the next lower one. Thus, in the key of C:

Ex. 98

C VII_7

It is therefore, *in sound,* the embodiment of a square, which presents exactly the same appearance (sound) from every point of view, so that its component intervals are not distinguishable one from another. (You will observe, however, that while the first three spaces are all minor thirds, the uppermost one, into the octave, is an augmented second—a♭ to b♮. And that is precisely what supplies the chord with its array of transformations; for, since the intervals all *sound* alike, it follows that *any one* of the minor thirds may assume the identity of an augmented second—by altering the notation, of course.)

The conclusions to be drawn from this are: (1) that the chord in all its forms, fundamental and inverted, retains the *same sound;* (2) that one cannot determine which of its four tones is the leading-tone, until one hears its resolution into its tonic; (3) *that whatever any one of its tones may be, each one in turn may be; each one of the four tones may be a leading-tone, or the seventh or ninth, of the elusive chord.*

Notations of the Diminished-Seventh Chords

Of course—and upon this circumstance all the wonderful properties of the chord hinge—when we exchange one of its tones, as leading-tone, for another of its tones, as leading-tone again, we *change the key* and must therefore change the *notation,* enharmonically.

For this chord, like the chameleon, adjusts its notation (its color) to the key (the object) upon which it stands, without altering its substance (its sound). Thus, leading-tone B (shown at "a"); leading-tone D (shown at "b"); leading-tone F or E♯ (shown at "c"); and leading-tone G♯ or A♭ (shown at "d"):

Ex.99

Test this at the piano. And verify the enharmonic changes in *notation,* rendered imperative by the shifts of key. We had to call the original F an E♯, and the A♭ a G♯, for convenience at least, since neither F nor A♭ are so likely to appear as leading-tones, in our community of keys. Our chameleon must at least play fair and stay in the ring of keys in common use. Note that the diminished seventh here used is the same in *sound* in every case; only the notation is altered, to conform to the several keys.

This gives us already eight different resolutions of the diminished-7th chord, as *Dominant* harmony; four into the minor tonics, and four into the corresponding major ones.

The Diminished-Seventh as Altered Chord

But we are not done. As if to render confusion doubly confused, we cannot escape the other facts we have discovered, namely, that besides its *legitimate* location as VII_7, on the leading-tone, the diminished-seventh chord appears very frequently as an altered chord. If you will take the trouble to review our fourth chapter, you will find, in Exs. 28 and 31, an array of altered chords, and will discover certain diminished-seventh chords among them.

One of the commonest altered chords is the II_7 in major, with raised fourth and second steps; and this chord has the shape and sound of the diminished-seventh chord. Consequently, since our chameleon-chord is everywhere the selfsame harmonic structure, it follows that the VII_7 of minor, exhibited in Ex. 99, may be (and of course very often is) interchanged with the altered II_7 of a major key. For example:

Ex. 100

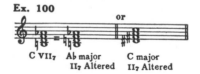

C VII_7 Ab major   C major
II_7 Altered II_7 Altered

The first chord, here, is the same diminished seventh that was demonstrated in Ex. 99; and it is shown also in its harmonic identity as II_7 of Ab major, with raised second and fourth steps (B♮ and D♮). The chord, in C major, is also seen.

This new chord is a member of the second-dominant class, and therefore it contains not the leading-tone but the *tonic note* (according to our tabulation in the foregoing). And this tonic is the uppermost note of the chord in its fundamental form—as chord of the seventh. This provides a quick method of recognizing it; and, inasmuch as a diminished-seventh chord is made up of intervals of three half-steps up, or down, or sidewise, you might reverse the process of the original VII_7 and build this altered chord *downward* from the tonic, instead of upward from the leading-tone. But do not lose sight of the simple method of "spelling" a chord, upward from its *root* in successive thirds. The

II_7 in C must be spelled, as far as its *letters* are concerned, beginning with the second step as root, D-F-A-C. Whatever alterations occur, merely inflect certain of these letters, with accidentals, but do not alter the letters themselves; the II_7 of C consists *always* of the letters D-F-A-C.

Here again, of course, *each one* of the four tones of the chord may successively be taken as a tonic note, resulting in the same metamorphoses that are witnessed in Ex. 99. This chord resolves into the I of its key, as shown in the following table of its ambiguities: (a) tonic C; (b) tonic E♭; (c) tonic F♯ or G♭; (d) tonic A:

C maj. II_7 I   E♭ major   F♯ maj.   G♭ maj.   A maj.

Test this also at the piano and verify the enharmonic changes in notation.

Further, the diminished-seventh chord appears, also very frequently, as IV_7 in minor, with raised fourth and sixth steps. Here, again, the *tonic* note is present—but next below the uppermost note; and this chord also resolves into the I of its key. And of course the chord admits of the selfsame metamorphoses. Thus: (a) tonic A; (b) tonic C; (c) tonic D♯ or E♭; (d) tonic F♯:

A min. IV_7 I   C minor   D♯ min.   E♭ min.   F♯ minor

This is the same diminished-seventh chord that is manipulated in Ex. 101. Test it at the piano, and compare it with Ex. 101.

These chords, like the preceding VII_7, yield, together, eight new resolutions (or keys), four in major and four in minor.

I almost dread to betray to you that the resources of the diminished-seventh chord are not yet exhausted: there is still another altered chord which exhibits this structural shape, and that is the VI_7 in major, with raised first and sixth steps. It resolves to the V_7 always (not directly into the tonic), and therefore, since the V_7 resolves itself into both major and minor tonics, there are again eight other keys of which this diminished seventh is a member—four majors and four corresponding minors.

This chord contains the *dominant* note as a distinctive feature, and it lies at the top of the chord as uppermost note. For example: (a) dominant, G; (b) dominant, B♭; (c) dominant, C♯; (d) dominant, D♭; (e) dominant E:

Ex. 103

Thus we obtain, in all, twenty-four legitimate resolutions of any one of the diminished-seventh chords, into every one of the twelve major and twelve minor keys, thus covering, *at one tonal point*, the whole range of our tonality.

I have not used the same one for each of the foregoing examples, but that is of no consequence; because what any one diminished seventh can do, they can all do. They are exactly alike in their ambiguous disposition. All depends solely upon the notation.

It is a wise dispensation of Providence that there are *only three* diminished-seventh chords in music which *differ in sound*: one with B in it, one with B♯ (or C), and one with C♯ (or D♭); the next higher one, with D in it, is the same as the first-mentioned —and so on. These three are manipulated in Ex. 99, Ex. 101 (102), and Ex. 103. But you must realize that all of these twenty-four resolutions may be effected from *each one* of the diminished-seventh chords. Instead of making a complete table, as I was tempted to do, I would suggest that you win and enjoy the triumph of doing this yourself, and for this purpose use the diminished-seventh chord of E minor, D♯-F♯-A-C. Do not fail to realize that the twenty-four different resolutions involve changes in the *notation* of the chord.

To these twenty-four "resolutions" we must add the progressions from one diminished-seventh chord directly into another, chromatically, of course. Thus (A) Beethoven, Op. 10, No. 3; (B) Chopin, Op. 45:

Ex. 104

The notation of the diminished-seventh chords, in such chromatic successions, is generally optional and approximate; for they represent "passing modulations," wherein each key is too brief to assert itself.   This condition renders futile the basic rule of all notation, namely, that it depends absolutely upon the prevailing *key;* here no key "prevails" long enough to exercise authority. It will be seen that the keys, in Ex. 104, are at least all closely interrelated; and it is safe to conclude that these two masters employed theoretically unassailable notation.

Classic Examples of the Use of Diminished-Seventh Chords

In concluding the fascinating story of this adventuresome, rather baffling and yet most lovable of chords, it will be of interest to the reader to cite a few memorable instances of the use of the diminished-seventh chords in the works of classic masters:

Ex. 105

In order to apprehend fully the nature and effect of the diminished-seventh chords in these excerpts, they should be studied not as isolated passages but in connection with the surrounding measures and phrases. Ex. 105, (A), is from Beethoven's Sonata, Op. 7, the third movement, second part; play the whole Allegro.

"B" is from the second movement of his Op. 10, No. 3, measures 23-26; see also measures 6-7 of the same movement:

"C" is from Beethoven's *Appassionata* Sonata, Op. 57, the end of the second movement and beginning of the finale; play also the following fifteen measures.

"D" is from the first movement of Beethoven's Symphony No. 8, measures 52-61; play the preceding six measures, and the six which follow this example:

"E" is from Beethoven's Violin Concerto, first movement, measures 65-71; note the enharmonic change in measure 69; the b♯ becomes c♮, and the first diminished seventh chord (the VI₇

of D, with raised first and sixth steps) is deflected into the legitimate VII₇ of E minor; compare Ex. 103, in the foregoing, with Ex. 99.

"F" is from the Bb minor prelude in the first book of Bach's "Well Tempered Clavichord"—measures 4 and 3 from the end. Bach (his name is the German word for "brook," but Beethoven said it should be "Meer," the ocean) uses every chord and tone-combination ever conceived by man or angel, of course, and always with the discrimination of true genius; so, while he is somewhat less addicted to this "most wonderful chord in music" than was, for example, Beethoven, he (Bach) did not underestimate its marvelous qualities nor fail to give it generous room in his scheme of chords and keys.

"G" is the famous *Venus* theme from Wagner's "Tannhäuser," the measures in the *Overture* which follow the lengthy *Pilgrims' Hymn,* at the opening of the opera (the *Allegro*). I have altered the notation of G natural to F double-sharp for the benefit of the student, who need not be misled by those motives of *convenience* which quite often influence a composer in his choice of accidentals:

"H" is that suggestive passage from the "Academic Overture" of Brahms, measures 17-23, in which the master ventures (very contrary to his usual unyielding adherence to the spirit of absolute music) to make a droll allusion to the "Salamander"-ceremony of the German student. No other chord than the diminished-seventh could have served his whimsical purpose better.

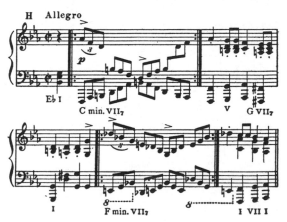

Such specimens of the diminished-seventh chord in classic music might be multiplied a thousand fold, and I cannot claim to have singled out the most characteristic or significant ones. They, in common with this whole chapter, open up one of the most prolific, instructive and at the same time alluring fields of tonal creation; and the reader will scarcely need to be urged to conduct a quest for the diminished-seventh chords and make studious testings of their properties and effects, in the music that occupies his attention.

SELF-TEST QUESTIONS

1. Which is the most wonderful chord in music?
2. Which qualities assure it this distinction?
3. Define the origin of the diminished-seventh chord: to which mode does it legitimately belong? to which chord family? on which step of the scale?
4. How does it divide the chromatic octave?
5. What conclusions are drawn from this peculiar formation?
6. What defines the notation of a diminished-7th chord?
7. In what other harmonic capacity and location do diminished-7th chords appear in the key?
8. How many resolutions can any single diminished-7th chord make?
9. What other progressions are possible, besides these "resolutions"?
10. Do classic masters use this chord freely?

CHAPTER 11

Counterpoint. The Interweaving of Melodies

Our word, "Counterpoint," is derived from the Latin *punctus contra punctum* (literally, "note against note"), a term which was adopted by early ecclesiastic music enthusiasts who, in the solitude of their cloisters, abstracted from the preoccupations of the secular world and always devoting much of their time and energy to studious pursuits, gave earnest attention to the music of the church.

About one thousand years ago they began to conduct experiments under this title, at first crude and uncertain, but destined to lead in time directly to the new and marvelous era of musical art in which we now rejoice. Aiming to enrich and widen the scope of the simple, though, in their way, appropriate and impressive monodies and chants of the ritual service, they conceived the happy idea of increasing their limited supply of established melodies by *adding a new melody* to certain of the given ones— doubtless more from scholastic than from religious impulse. The new melody was thus "generated" out of the given one by simply setting a new accordant tone to each tone of the latter, "note against note."

This was several centuries before the era of the harmonic (chord) system; but, since these pioneers were guided by the same instinct of *harmonious* union which alone could assure acceptable results, it was through their experiments that our modern harmonic system was started upon its course of evolution and development.

It is a somewhat curious phenomenon in music history that in this very respect evolution seemed to move in the reverse direction, counterpoint thus preceding harmony; whereas it is now universally conceded that contrapuntal discipline and achievement *follow* that of harmony; that, in a word, counterpoint is merely a higher, more advanced grade of harmony. There is no evading this conclusion; for, since "the chords are the source and genesis of *all* music," their dominion is as absolute in the polyphonic (contrapuntal) as in the homophonic (harmonic) sphere.

Homoph'ony and Polyph'ony

The distinction between these two basic varieties of musical composition, the homo-phonic and the poly-phonic, may be thus defined: in the homophonic style (ho-moph'-ony) there is, as the word indicates, only one outstanding melodic line, the tune, which all the other tones serve chiefly to accompany and support; this style is exemplified in our church hymns and in the very great majority of vocal and instrumental pieces that you hear (for instance, the *Melody in F* of Rubinstein, or the "Songs without Words" of Mendelssohn). In the polyphonic style (po-lyph'-ony), on the other hand, there are two or more distinct melodies, sounding simultaneously and contrived to agree with each other by virtue of the regulations of counterpoint; types of this less common but more elaborate and scholarly style are all the fugues and most of the preludes in Bach's "Well-tempered Clavichord." I am tempted to offer a homely illustration of this distinction, though it is perhaps a little far-fetched: the simile involves two images, (1) a stone wall, and (2) a row of telegraph poles and wires. In our wall, as symbol of the homophonic style, the stones represent the *chords,* and these constitute the total contents; there is no other *line* (melody) present than that described by the top of the wall—like the tune, or air, of our church hymns, sung by the uppermost voice, the soprano. (In the "melody" of Rubinstein this line, or tune, is not at the top, but runs along inside of the chords; in the "Songs without Words" it is almost invariably the uppermost line, which seems to be its proper place—like the cream at the top of the milk jar.)

In the second one of our two images, symbolizing the polyphonic style, the telegraph poles represent the chords, and the 2, 3 or more wires stretched from pole to pole are the lines or melodies; these are separate strands, each carrying its particular message, and yet all are held together by their contact with the poles. The latter (the chords) do, by their order, surely give direction to the wires and support them; and though the poles have no weightier share than this, in the message delivered, it is none the less certain that, without this direction and support, the wires would trail on the ground in a tangled mess.

Counterpoint a Process, Not a Style

As an inducement to accuracy of thought, you must be reminded that the term "counterpoint" refers to a *technical process* and not to a style of composition. Do not call a fugue "counterpoint"; fugues pertain to the polyphonic (many-voiced) style, while counterpoint is merely the method, the tools, employed in creating this style. Likewise, hymn tunes are not "harmony," but are examples of the homophonic (single-melody) style, created through the agency of chords. At the same time, even the most punctilious of us are rather inclined to extend the term to include the product as well as the tools; and, after all, generally speaking, there is no danger of misapprehension.

The Object of Counterpoint

The technical aim of the contrapuntal process is, then, to derive, or, more properly, to generate, a new melody out of a given one. It is therefore, apparently, a purely mechanical process —the *artistic* application of a prosaic mathematical operation. And yet, if executed in the right way, by a mind that is fully sensible of melodic values and skilled in the manifold devices of contrapuntal technic, the results will be thoroughly musical, admirably refined and worthy of fullest recognition.

To make this clear, I submit a specimen of counterpoint, applied to as unpromising an example of melodic monotony and uncouthness as can well be found—the first half of our worthy old campaign ditty, *Yankee Doodle:*.

The "given" melody, *Yankee Doodle,* is placed in the lower voice, and to this is "added" a *new* melody, contrapuntally adjusted to, or generated out of, the given one. I have chosen this homespun, "unmelodious" old tune as a good test of what counterpoint can elicit from the most unpromising specimens; fine fruit is often gathered from scrubby, misshapen trees. At all events, this dear old homely melody was probably never in better company. Now, in order to appreciate just what is gained by this process, it is necessary to separate the two melodies and sing *the new one alone,* without reference to the given one.

It must be clearly understood that the above attempt is only one of very many possible solutions; a skillful contrapuntist (akin to crossword and jig-saw fanatics) could cypher out a hundred, perhaps many hundred, different "new" melodies as associates to *Yankee Doodle;* for, by utilizing the resources of rhythm, modulation, passing-notes, different registers, and the general devices of melodic delineation, the number of legitimate, more or less acceptable and valuable *new* melodies that may be thus generated out of any given melody is practically unlimited. Hence the extreme importance of counterpoint to the composer, not only as a means of multiplying his thematic resources and increasing his melodic supply, but also as the significant technical act of associating independent melodic lines—the interweaving of distinct melodic strands.

The mandate, "note against note," need not be construed rigorously; if applied, strictly, to each separate note of the phrase, the result must be absolutely coincident rhythm in the two melodies; therefore, in favor of greater freedom and variety, two (or even more) notes may occasionally confront one of the given tones—as witnessed in the foregoing example (and in Ex. 110).

In order to emphasize the distinction between the two basic types of composition, homoph'-ony and polyph'-ony, we might insert here an illustration of the purely homophonic (harmonic) treatment of *Yankee Doodle,* with the tune at the *top,* by way of comparison with the polyphonic version in Ex. 106:

Here there is only one single vital melodic line; whereas in Ex. 106, *two* independent melodies are interwoven.

Albeit this essay is not, and could not be, designed as a "lesson," as an exposition of the manifold rules and regulations of contrapuntal technic, it is necessary to mention at least the more fundamental conditions of this complex art. First of all, let us record the three absolutely vital requisites of good polyphony:

(1) Perfect melody in each part.
(2) Harmonious agreement of the melodies with each other.
(3) Sufficient independence of each part to insure an association of actually *different* melodies.

(1) The conditions of "perfect melody" are not easy to define offhand. As stated in our sixth chapter, melody is a most mysterious agent, whose grades of propriety and excellence depend largely upon indefinable factors. But melody possesses sufficient obvious traits to enable every musically minded person to discriminate and detect its quality; the majority of musicians will agree, tacitly, that such and such a melody is good, or bad, or indifferent; that it does, or does not, reveal those qualities of smoothness, interest and naturalness which distinguish the "good" melodies from the poor ones. And it is self-evident that no amount of contrapuntal acuteness can disguise or excuse faulty or awkward melodic movements in any of the interlocking melodic lines.

(2) It goes without saying that the separate melodies must *harmonize* with each other; else we should have, instead of a congenial, unanimous community, a rabble of discordant elements. And this is the chief concern of the contrapuntist and the source of all his "rules."

(3) Unless the melodies differ sufficiently to identify themselves severally, we have missed the point completely; mere duplication is not actual multiplication. A person cannot establish a partnership with his own self; even twins should be distinguishable.

As stated, the most important technical requirement is that of harmonious union; and that is precisely the juncture at which harmony enters so inevitably into the contrapuntal operations. From this primitive point of view, the problem assumes a simple aspect and reveals a code of "laws" which are easy to grasp and to apply. These rules relate, fundamentally, to two-voice counterpoint.

Rules of Two-Voice Counterpoint

The most harmonious intervals, involved in the primary chord-formations, are the *third,* the *sixth,* and the *octave* (or unison). These, therefore, are the intervals employed in all the basic adjustments of "note against note"; they are the staple intervals of polyphony. Their application may be thus roughly illustrated; "A" being the given melody, "B" this melody with an added voice below, "C" other correct versions, and "D" and "E" faulty versions:

"B" and "C," though different versions, are both correct; from which the conclusion is drawn that these three perfectly good intervals (3, 6, 8) may be interchanged in many ways, with varying melodic results; and it is precisely *this interchange* which constitutes the chief problem of the contrapuntist. He may always depend upon the validity of one or the other of his 3, 6 and 8, but the question he must ponder is *when* to use 3, *when* to use 6, or *when* to use 8. The answer to this—the *choice* between the three "good" intervals—is referred directly to the basic laws: perfect melody and independence of the voices. "D" is faulty, notwithstanding the good quality of the intervals, because the added melody (lower voice) is too jerky, and involves incorrect chord conditions. "E" is faulty, since the two parts move so parallel that the added one is but little more than a duplication of the given part, and consequently not independent.

But besides these three staple intervals there are a few slightly less euphonious ones that, for the sake of greater freedom and increased possibilities, may be used; namely, an occasional, single, perfect fifth may alternate with the "good" intervals; also, any interval contained in the dominant-seventh (or ninth) chord. The interval to be most carefully shunned is the perfect fourth, on a full beat, or when in any degree prominent. For example, in the following, "A" is acceptable but "B" faulty:

When the added part moves more quickly than the given one
(as conducive to more pronounced independence) *any* intervals
may be inserted as brief passing or neighboring notes. Being
thus "inharmonic," they are not subject to the fundamental rules,
but serve only as useful embellishments of the essential intervals.
It is self-evident that they should be brief and smooth. "A" and
"B" in the following are two notes against one; "C" and "D"
are three notes against one; "E" is four notes against one.

Note that versions "A" and "D" are based upon the same
essential intervals used in Ex. 108, B. Version "E" differs from
these at one point only. Version "C" depends chiefly upon the
regular sequential formation of the added voice—an excellent
device. Version "D" and "E" introduce changes of key.

These examples represent, intentionally, the simplest, most
obvious solutions. Very many others are possible, of course; and
it may be necessary to remind those of our readers who look for

particularly elaborate, striking, or "trick" solutions here, that I am addressing myself to the average music lover, not to the futuristic expert.

Now review Ex. 106, and verify the application there made of our contrapuntal regulations. And to this it will prove illuminating to add some specimens of the contrapuntal methods of that giant of polyphony, Bach ("A," Vol. I, "Well-Tempered Clavichord"; "B," Vol. II):

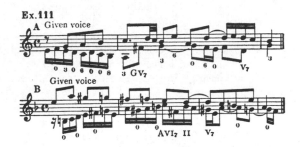

As already stated, all the principles of contrapuntal practice are embodied in two-voice structure; and, while their uses are identified with the polyphonic style, they may be, and very often are, employed in purely homophonic sentences. For while this latter style is distinguished by the evidence of only one essential melody, placed naturally at the top, it is impossible to overlook the presence of at least one other "melodic" tone-line, represented most commonly by the *bass-voice,* and defined, inescapably, by contrapuntal conditions. Thus, for a random example: in the *Finale* of Beethoven's "Sonata, Op. 79," it is clear that, having conceived the upper melody as thematic tune, he fixed the bass part in contrapuntal agreement with the former:

Three- and Four-voice Counterpoint

Although we have seen that two associated independent melodies involve primarily the entire apparatus of counterpoint, it is true that the more complex and amazing feats seem to demand at least three, and often four or more such simultaneous interwoven melodic lines.   But, the moment we advance beyond the two voices, we enter a realm of tone-association where the influence and domination of the *chords* are unmistakably and inevitably asserted.   For without sufficiently obvious and frequent chord-nodes (accordant bodies), the most vital requirement—"harmonious union"—must almost certainly be sacrificed.   The best we can do, in 3 or 4 voice counterpoint, is to impart as much independent individuality as possible to each separate melodic line (by means of rhythmic and melodic contrast, or by thematic authority), while adjusting the whole to the essential chord-basis. One illustration, from Bach's Vol. II, *Fugue in D,* will suffice:

This is an unexcelled specimen of masterly four-part polyphony, such as few besides Bach could create.   The total effect is surely ascribable to the singularly clear and normal chord-progression; within which, the equally clear concept of *four interwoven melodies,* each one a complete and perfect tone-line by itself, is fully assured—play each one separately.   The "given melody," or theme of the whole fugue, is intonated by the alto voice (the lower one in the "right hand"), and this imparts unchallenged validity to that voice; the same thematic melody follows, in the uppermost part (soprano), thus vesting equal authority in this part; for though it is similar to the alto, it is not mere duplication, since it stands in a different rhythmic position.   The tenor voice (the upper one in the "left hand") confirms its thematic identity by a fragment of the theme, and then fulfils its purpose in an unconstrained melodic progression.   The lowermost voice (bass) is a perfect model of independent melodic and rhythmic delineation. Play the whole fugue; this excerpt appears in measures 14-16.

Noteworthy Examples of Polyphony

Classic literature of every type teems with specimens of fine counterpoint, of which a few noteworthy ones are here recorded:

"A" is from the *C major Fugue* in Book I of Bach's "Well-Tempered Clavichord." It is remarkable in that there is scarcely a note in all the four voices, which is not dictated by the theme. This might seem to cancel the individuality of the several parts; but it establishes the equally valuable attribute of "equality"; like Ex. 113, it is a sign of confirmation and not of mere duplication, since the theme appears everywhere on different beats.

"B" is from Book II, *Fugue 8*. The theme is intonated simultaneously in two of the voices, but in the tenor it is traced in contrary motion (upside down), every movement being exactly reversed. Note the perfect melodic conduct of the other two voices.

"C" is from Book II, *Fugue 2*. Here again, almost every note is dictated by the theme; in the inner voice the notes appear in double length (augmentation); in the lower voice the theme is upside down. "D" is the famous contrapuntal association of three outstanding thematic factors in Wagner's *Overture* to "Die Meistersinger"—near the end. The upper part, marked "W," is a portion of Walther's *Prize-song;* the lowest voice carries the motives of the "Mastersingers," marked "M"; the inner parts consist of the *Fanfare* or *Banner* motive, marked "B," which signalizes the momentous "singing-test."

"E" is from the third piano sonata of Brahms (finale). The "theme" is placed in the upper part in its legitimate rhythmic form, while the lower voice presents it in three-fold diminution (quickened rhythm) as far as it can.

It should interest and will surely stimulate and edify the student to watch for similar examples of striking counterpoint in such polyphonic literature as he encounters in his musical activities.

SELF-TEST QUESTIONS

1. Explain the derivation of our word "counterpoint."
2. Define the distinction between the homophonic and polyphonic styles.
3. What is the technical aim of counterpoint?
4. Define the three vital requisites of good polyphony.
5. Which are the three basic intervals of all contrapuntal practice? Why?
6. Which other, less euphonious, intervals are used?
7. What is permitted when the added voice moves more quickly than the given one?

8. How is counterpoint naturally employed in homophonic (harmonic) sentences?
9. Describe the qualities in Ex. 113 (from Bach) which stamp this an unexcelled example of masterly counterpoint.

CHAPTER 12

How the Composer Goes to Work
What "Form" is in Music

The composer, like the architect, must begin his task with some definite plan in mind. That of the composer will be less vivid, less definite, than the design of the builder. But it is not a whit less important. What is "form" in music?

When the word "form" is mentioned in connection with music, it conjures up, in the mind of a large number of music lovers, the vision of an iron foundry where the prepared "forms" stand ready for the reception of the molten metal which is to take on the shape unalterably predestined by these "forms." That idea, as applied to music, is just as false as the opposite view would be: namely, that the molten mass might better be simply poured out over the floor, in haughty disdain of any guiding and controlling pattern. To be sure, there is nothing in musical discipline that is as binding as the founder's "forms"; but we naturally demand sufficiently distinct outlines to inform us whether we are gazing upon a shapely tree or upon an elephant.

The Merging Arts

The arts of architecture, sculpture and painting are almost, if not completely, dominated by the outward physical forms which they are to embody; and, while they are expected to contain a certain intangible poetic or mystic significance which confers true artistic worth upon them, they would be unthinkable without their definite external formative lines. Even poetry differentiates itself from prose and general literature through established elements of form, its meters, its rhythms and rhymes, its stanza, sonnet, canto. These, it is true, are subservient to the actual poetic contents, and they are so elastic that they exert no great influence upon the latter. It was very natural, practically inevitable, that music should appropriate many of these formative elements of poetry, for the art of music is far more closely allied with that of poetry than with any other of the sister arts. Music has always gone hand in hand with poetry, and was born and reared under its influence—witness the folk-songs, the music of the church, and

142

the superabundance of songs and vocal settings generally. Only in the instrumental domain does music seem to renounce *some portion* of this poetic guardianship.

Ever since chaos was conquered, there has been no phenomenon in nature without form; even the unfettered breakers on the seashore and the fantastic sunset clouds have their shapes. Music will not be exempted from its obligation to comply with the law; it must assume regulated forms, consistent with its specific substance, ethereal though this "substance" be.

Form without Shape

Now, there is a subtle distinction between form and *shape,* and perhaps it is the imperfect conception of this difference that has led to the prejudice, in many modern minds, against any conceivable restrictions upon the movements of so shapeless, incorporeal a medium of soul-communication as music is. Shape refers to the external contour only; form strikes deeper, and is defined as "orderly arrangement, symmetry." Music is a vague, mysterious, intangible medium, and can have no *shape;* but it is precisely by reason of this utter lack of tangible properties that music stands in need, indispensably, of that "orderly arrangement" which is the essence of *form.* And that is why music, or rather the presentation, the methods of expression employed in music, have been wisely hedged about by a system of controlling, restricting, defining regulations (to the disgust of a certain class of critics), designed to prevent its escape, so to speak, from the domain of reason and common sense. This hedge is by no means a hide-bound provision; it is flexible enough, and there are crevices enough to permit the spirit of music to expand and soar aloft with that freedom which is its precious birthright, and with that flaming vitality that inspires and thrills humanity as perhaps no other revelation of divine purpose has ever been able to do.

Landmarks in Tone

To repeat: it is exactly because of the unsubstantial, volatile nature of music that it became necessary to fix certain landmarks which provide for it a recognizable stability, and transform it into an object of systematic evolution and practicability. The first factor to be established, by nature herself, was the family of tones known as the *key,* with the *scale* that emerges from it. Then came the *chords,* and then the *tonality* or community of keys. These units are, comparatively speaking, stationary, and they furnish the necessary basic points of departure. They are somewhat analogous to the pillars and posts of our ethereal tone-edifice.

But its own inherent vitality imparted *motion* to the mass, and, with it, the principles of *rhythm* came into play; and it is just at this point that the regulated system known as *musical form* begins.

The Essential Attributes of Musical Art

Let us first define some of the most vital and essential attributes of musical composition. There are two which concern the *technical,* and two others which are implicated in the *spiritual* realm of music. We must consider first of all the technical constituents, for technic is a matter of foremost importance. There is no earthly use in having something to say, if one does not know how to say it.

The first of these technical attributes is *continuity;* and the second is *thematic manipulation.*

(1) By continuity is meant the never-failing evidence of purpose, the conception and arrangement of each member as a recognizable progressive growth out of the members which precede it. No meaningless episodes, no halting, no capricious, silly insertion of some foreign passage, but the unbroken certainty of a continuous plan or idea which runs through the whole piece like a silver bar, holding all its members inseparably together as a unified total. This is the distinctive sign, the earmark of genius, and it is perhaps nowhere in music literature more admirably exhibited than in the symphonies of Beethoven. The classic master "sticks to his text."

(2) By thematic manipulation is meant the legitimate exploitation of the manifold possibilities stored up within the simple tones of the themes or motives. Every piece of music must have a *theme,* just as every essay, every book, must have a title; and the most masterly essay or sermon is that one in which every concealed, often unsuspected, meaning of the title or text is truthfully and recognizably recorded. This need not involve monotony nor petty juggling. There will usually be more than one theme, perhaps a number of subsidiary motives which assure additional variety and contrast. And of course the more attractive and pregnant the themes are, the better; it is not exactly wise to accept "any old theme"; the composer usually awaits a moment of "inspiration," and is thoroughly jubilant when he can assure his friends that he "has struck a stunning good theme." The theme

may, like so many of those of Brahms, seem uninviting at a first hearing. All the better, maybe; it is the composer's problem to unfold from it disguised beauties and unexpected resources. One stands amazed before the harvest garnered from such unpromising themes as, for instance, that in the *Finale* of the "Symphony in D minor" of César Franck, or the *Finale* of Brahms' "Symphony No. 3" (see Ex. 115, B).

Manipulating the Theme

Now this, be it well understood, is, as already stated, a purely *technical* process, and one may question its importance. But *technic* is a most precious, vitally necessary thing, a factor that vindicates its worth in music to a great degree in precisely these operations of thematic manipulation. If the artist is inexorably bound to "stick to his text," he must compensate himself by ringing sufficient changes upon it to banish monotony and keep his hold upon the interest of his hearer.

I am tempted to cite a few striking instances of this operation, "thematic manipulation":

"A" is from Brahms' *Intermezzo*, Op. 117, No. 3; "B" is from the Finale of his Third Symphony; "C" is from the third movement of his Second Symphony; and "D" is from Beethoven's Fifth Symphony.

(3) A third attribute of musical art, is that poetic, dramatic, indefinable ethereal quality which breathes into the dormant tonal body the breath of life, and endows the music with a soul. This, as stated, has nothing to do with the *structural* plan in itself. At the same time, the true composer whose aim is high and whose purpose is serious, cannot ignore the influence of this spiritual agency, no matter how deeply he may be engrossed in the technical exigencies of his task.

Keyboard Consciousness

The superficial "composer" (?) who claws his "music" (?) out of the keyboard, and concerns himself with nothing more important than the stringing together of a series of unrelated "pretty" or "brilliant" episodes, produces an abortion, without life, totally devoid of a *raison d'être*. No master "composes" at the piano, any more than "at the orchestra." For true, enduring composition is an exceedingly exacting task, which enlists both the head and the heart—probably three-fourths head; it is a task which enjoins complete abstraction from every material auxiliary.

It is said that Chopin conceived much of his music at the keyboard: if this be true (it is well authenticated) I should account for it by the fact that he possessed such alert, exceptionally rapid perceptive power that he simply played, apparently simultaneously, his mental concept and its pianistic setting; and it must not be overlooked that Chopin's marvellously beautiful, though rarely profound music (in the classical sense) was almost exclusively conceived *for* (and no doubt to some extent *at*) the piano. Every virtuoso knows how admirably Chopin's music is adjusted to the keyboard, and how much easier it is to play (for that very reason), than, say, a sonata of Mozart or Beethoven—or Brahms.

(4) And, finally, there is a fourth attribute, that of attractiveness, loveliness, *inherent tonal beauty*. No sane being honestly prefers an ugly face to a beautiful one. How one's heart expands with joy over such musical gems as the *Andante* of Sibelius' "Symphony No. 1," or the ineffably lovely *Juliet* episode in Tchaikovsky's "Tone-poem"; or the first theme in Brahms' "Second Symphony"—also the third movement of the same symphony (Ex. 115, C.), not to mention the numberless exquisite measures

in all the works of Schumann, or the indescribable beauty of so many of Schubert's conceptions!

The question arises, "What is the attitude of the modern composer toward these four vital attributes?" There is no reason why even the most ultramodern music should not adhere to these conditions, and no reason why, as long as it does so, one should be justified in condemning it, bag and baggage. Unprejudiced analysis of modern music shows that it has continuity, displays astounding skill in thematic manipulation, and is usually impelled by some very obvious emotional and spiritual, even mystic, aims. The attribute which seems to be rather wilfully repudiated is that of tonal beauty. Modern music is almost preponderantly ugly—or it impresses many of us as being so. This may be our own fault. As our ears become accustomed to the discordant mess, or as our conception of "tonal beauty" undergoes perhaps inevitable modification, we may find this modern music as beautiful as the cherished classic types.

The Structural Factors of Composition

Now let us turn to a practical review of the concrete structural factors upon which musical form must depend. The basic unit of all musical formations is the single *tone*. A brief succession of two, three or more tones constitutes the *figure*. Two or three such figures form the motive or *phrase-member*. Two or three members make a *phrase,* which is the smallest complete musical sentence (usually four measures long). Two phrases form the *period* (eight measures) ; and two connected periods make a *double-period* (generally sixteen measures).

Beyond this, the primary forms rarely extend; a decisive, strong *cadence* brings this portion of the piece to a fairly complete stop, as a rule. This portion is known as a *Part*.

This table is only approximate. Melodic conception is so incalculable that the smaller subdivisions of the phrase are often not definable; frequently the whole phrase consists of one unbroken member. The demarcations of these factors are analogous to the punctuation marks in our written language—the commas, semicolons, colons and full stops; and they are always plain enough to the intelligent musician. In Ex. 116 they are very clear, since the "joints" are fixed by the rests, equivalent to commas; the semi-cadence in the fourth measure equals a semicolon; the perfect cadence in the eighth measure is a full stop. These details are all shown in the following, from Beethoven's "Sonata No. 2."

The *figure* in this example, the index of the whole, occurring six times, consists of five notes. Two of the figures form the first *member,* to which a second member, partly similar and partly independent, is added, to complete the first four-measure *phrase,* called the antecedent, because its cadence is not a complete one and therefore involves a "consequent" phrase to round out the entire *period.* Note the similarity in the construction of these two phrases, and, at the same time, the contrast in their *harmonic* plan, the antecedent being based largely upon the tonic, the consequent upon the dominant, harmony. Note the complete, final, perfect cadence at the end of the period. This definitely concludes the first Part. Note also that this part is repeated.

The first Part, in short sentences, may consist of one phrase only; but it is most commonly a period, and, in broader design, a double-period, though this is somewhat rare.

The (usually) heavy cadence at the end of the first part is like a corner, from which a new direction is taken—*into the second part.* The latter is likely to be a little longer than the first, and, if it terminates with a complete "perfect" (tonic) cadence in *the original key,* it ends the piece; and such a structural design is called the *Two-part* form.

But two-part forms are rare. They are encountered only in small designs—as in some of our church hymns or simple folksongs. (*Home, Sweet Home* is an example of the two-part form.) Of the 48 "Songs without Words" of Mendelssohn, *only one* (No. 6) is a two-part design.

Consequently, in the great majority of pieces in the "smaller" forms, the second part does *not* terminate the composition, but is followed by a *third part,* the structural object of which is very

definite and natural, namely: *the recurrence of the first part,* or of its main contents at least. This constitutes the *Three-part* form, illustrated in Ex. 117, which is the continuation of Ex. 116:

Note the manner in which the Second part confirms the First part (Ex. 116); its contents are very similar for a time, but the hands are exchanged. The whole first period of Part II is followed by two measures which merely "spin out" the foregoing motives; this is called an extension. Then, in phrase 3, the unexpected happens. An entirely *new* concept is introduced. This is unusual; but, since the second part, viewed broadly, is chiefly an (important) "interlude" between the first part and its recurrence as third part, it is considered logical enough to contrive a *portion* of its contents out of any material that is reasonably consistent with the rest, for the sake of effective contrast and freedom of conception. Phrase 4 partly corroborates phrase 3, and then the composer begins to think of getting back to his original key, and *preparing for the return to the beginning,* since the recurrence of the first period, as Part III, is the aim of the entire form. This episode is known as the returning passage. In this instance there can be no question of its beauty and effectiveness.

The Third part, here, is a *literal* recurrence of the First part. This is by no means an imperative procedure, nor is it even customary; often only the first few measures agree with the preceding version, while all the rest may be a fairly independent variation and extension of it.

What then follows—the last four measures—is a coda (or rather codetta, since it is so brief). It is the "tail" of the three-part design. Every dog has a tail, and, although it is perhaps not absolutely essential (witness the stupid habit of hacking it off), it is normal, useful and sometimes ornamental. The coda, being a "tail," will consist of the same stuff (musical contents) as the rest of the body. It is easy to recognize; anyone can see plainly where the body ends and the tail begins.

The Smaller, or Homophonic Forms

The Two-part and Three-part forms, with their occasional enlargement into a Five-part form, or into the minuet or march form and waltz form, are known as the *smaller,* or homophonic, forms of composition, and these are the ones most commonly employed in music. The Minuet consists of two independent, but connected, part-forms, the second one of which, called the Trio, is followed by a recurrence of the first one. See the entire third movement of Beethoven's "Sonata No. 2" (partly quoted in Exs. 116 and 117). The Waltz is a "group" of related part-forms, the final one of which returns to the beginning. Those of our readers who desire to acquire fuller cognizance of these basic structural principles will find convenient material in my edition of the "Songs without Words," wherein every detail of the form is indicated.

The Larger Forms

Of the larger structural designs, the three Rondos, the Sonatine and Sonata forms, but very little need be said here. They are identified with the sonata and symphony, and are, in a word, precisely the same as the smaller forms, merely expanded to broader dimensions. Their most distinctive feature is the presence of *two contrasted themes,* which alternate and coöperate with each other in manifold ways. (See my "Lessons in Music Form.")

Perhaps the most natural, logical and efficient methods employed by the far-sighted composer are those of *repetition,* and its allied companion, the *sequence.* The act of repetition may be applied to *any* factor: to the figure, the motive, the phrase, or the entire period or theme.

A repetition is sometimes literal, in which case the familiar "repeat marks" are used—as shown in Ex. 116. This proceeding, characteristic of the dances, marches, minuets and the like, exerts no other influence upon the form than merely to increase its length. If there is a change at the end of the sentence thus repeated, directions are given for a first and second ending, as in the first of the "Songs without Words" of Mendelssohn. Do not confound "repetition" and "recurrence." A repetition occurs *immediately;* a recurrence occurs after the insertion of some important section.

In its higher, more artistic application, however, the repetition is more or less elaborately varied, in order to produce "variety in unity" and elevate the simple act to the dignity of a positive contribution to the development and actual growth of the design. Beethoven, who seems to have assigned deeper significance to repetition than any other classic master, quite frequently repeats a member almost or quite literally, three or four (or even more) times in succession—as in this passage from his Fifth Symphony:

The methods of *variating* the repetitions are so numerous as to defy brief enumeration. They include changes in the melody, the rhythm, the register (Ex. 118, measures 9-12), the harmony, the mode (Ex. 121), and the style; it is a most fascinating object of quest for the student. For example, in Chopin's *Mazurka*, No. 32:

This four-measure phrase itself consists of a repetition of the two-measure member. Note the slight variations in the two outer voices.

The *sequence* is a reproduction (not a "repetition") of the melodic member, on either higher or lower steps. This shift entirely alters the situation, and therefore the sequence enters far more vitally into the constructive process. Like the repetition, it is sometimes exact, but often modified in various ways. For instance, in Chopin, Op. 55, No. 1:

Another extremely important structural device is that of *extension*—a "spinning out" of the preceding motive, which partly effaces the cadential impression and therefore does not constitute a new, progressive phrase. This was seen in Ex. 117, applied to the second phrase; and here is another interesting illustration, from Chopin's *Mazurka, No. 37:*

The whole constructive operation is here so clear that no comment is necessary.

Form in music is far too broad a subject for so brief a treatise; and yet I trust that you have gained a helpful general view of the problem of "How the Composer Goes to Work." To this I might add that a very thorough understanding of the fundamental processes can surely be acquired by a careful study of my analytic edition of the "Songs without Words," and this, I am convinced, will prove as fascinating as it is instructive.

SELF-TEST QUESTIONS

1. Which of the arts are dominated by physical forms?
2. With which of the sister arts is music most closely allied?
3. What is the distinction between "form" and "shape," and to which of these is music limited? Why?
4. Name the two attributes of music which concern technical processes.
5. Name two others, implicated in the spiritual realm.
6. Enumerate the half-dozen structural factors of music form.
7. What is a "part"?
8. What is the structural object of the third part?
9. What is a coda, or codetta?
10. Name the three larger forms.
11. What is their most distinctive feature?
12. Define the difference between *Repetition* and *Recurrence;* and between *Repetition* and *Sequence.*
13. Define *Extension.*

CHAPTER 13

The Merits and Methods of Analysis

With many sincere, conservative music lovers, and with a certain class of critics whose praiseworthy aim it is to envisage the art of tone as a broad, expansive horizon of glory and ecstasy, the mention of the word, "analysis," has something of the effect of a red cloth waved before the eyes of a bull. They esteem music as a divine revelation direct from Heaven, sacred in its isolated beauty as a perfect, untouchable, complete body-harmonious; and they resent, as sacrilege, any slashing into its precious substance, any attempt to peer within, any endeavor to discover the secret springs beneath the surface.

They have a perfect right to their opinions and inclinations, and they must be permitted to find their enjoyment and appreciation of music in their own way. But there is no more reason for discrediting serious systematic exploration of the manifold primary causes and physical factors involved in the consummation of the body-harmonious than there would be in denying a medical student the study of anatomy and its concomitant serious, beneficent, researches in the dissecting room of a college.

This latter liberal attitude is shared by quite as many equally sincere and conscientious musicians, and so we encounter, here again, wide diversity of opinion among intelligent music-lovers, critics and educators, in regard to the value and advantages of analysis to the student of music. As stated above, some reject it emphatically as being a too mechanical and narrow pursuit, devoid of the higher artistic stimulus, benumbing in its effects; while others recognize a very definite advantage in the conscientious analysis of the works of the masters, or of *any* standard musical literature—the advantage of probing, attentively, the methods of the masters, thereby acquiring a more complete and illuminating grasp upon the details of technic. Analysis of the *right sort* must lead, indisputably, to a fuller appreciation of the purport and contents of the composition.

The Good and Bad Features of Analysis

As usual, the truth probably lies midway between these two extreme views. Both are defensible: on the one hand, analysis does narrow our vision to a small segment of the problem, and is somewhat apt to divert our attention from the larger components which concern creation more significantly, as a whole, than does any fraction. But, on the other hand, analysis, like dissection and other laboratory activities, does ferret out important facts dealing with primary conditions, facts directed straightway toward that indispensable factor of all art and science—*technic*. It must therefore result in a more comprehensive understanding of the art-creation as a whole than can be obtained from the broader inspection which includes only the larger, ultimate items; and, while these latter are the true aim of the whole design, it cannot be denied that they are to be achieved only through thorough consideration of the multitude of units that compose the whole. One cannot claim really to know a piece of music unless one knows every particle of it.

While admitting the futility and hazards of that kind of analysis that concerns itself exclusively with the smaller units, I am convinced that true, *sensible* methods of analysis (only as a means to an end) must surely conduce to a fuller understanding of the master's implements and their application; must yield a plentiful harvest of information, and secure to the earnest student a more complete and stimulating knowledge of important factors than he can gain through purely mechanical study of text-books, with passive adherence to "rules," without the verification which living examples of their use can afford him.

But it must be a *sensible* course of analysis. It is quite true that there are different grades and methods, some helpful, and others not unlikely to be harmful. No one can countenance the misguided curiosity of the stupid boy who cut the drum open in order to discover where the noise came from; nor can any sensible person wax enthusiastic over the equally futile "analysis" by the girl who wasted precious moments counting the number of quarter notes in the first movement of a Beethoven sonata. At the same time, I cannot concur in the notion of some musical puritans who sneer at analysis as something fundamentally irreverent and antagonistic to creative labor. There need be no lack of reverence in subjecting an art creation to analysis; the quest merely supplements instinct (or intuition) with intelligence; both of these attributes are divine gifts, bestowed upon us *to be used*.

Taking for granted, then, that a great many of our readers are convinced of the utility, and the delight, of a study of musical analysis, I venture to outline a course of conduct, neither too superficial nor too inadvisedly minute, which will enable the student to obtain, easily and agreeably, a fuller insight into the motives which activate the composer in his structural arrangement of the musical material.

Analysis of the Form

It is wiser, in this research, to begin with the larger elements and work downward, than to start with the smaller details and work upward. Therefore, the first step should be an approximate definition of the factors that enter into the structural appointments of the piece in hand—that is, the *form*. To be sure, a certain general knowledge of musical form must be presupposed, and for that reason it may be necessary for you to review, more or less thoroughly, our twelfth chapter, since it is not practicable to restate here all the information there presented. But even this review may be dispensed with, if you will procure my analytic edition of Mendelssohn's "Songs without Words," wherein every detail of the form is carefully indicated. With the light to be gained from this material, the student will surely be able to extend his quest to all other smaller forms of classic, or, at least, respectable composition.

The student must limit himself, at least at present, strictly to the *smaller forms*. For these constitute the chief material that concerns him, and are almost invariably clear and simple in design and comparatively free from the numerous fascinating but confusing irregularities that make the analysis of the larger forms often extremely difficult.

The Cadences

Now, the most important element in musical structure (from the viewpoint of the novice in analysis) is, undoubtedly, the *cadence* or cadences. These he must learn, first of all, to recognize and to distinguish in their many different aspects and degrees of force. For there are at least three qualities of cadence in music, just as there are various degrees of separation in the punctuation marks of literature—namely: the perfect cadence, the semicadence, and the disguised (deferred, suppressed, averted or elided) cadence. These are the harmonic and rhythmic conjunctions that serve to separate the phrases and parts of the composition; literally, the punctuations of the sentences.

The perfect cadence, or full stop, is made upon the *tonic* harmony, on an accented beat (usually), with emphatic evidence of the chord-root (the key-note)—and preceded by the dominant harmony, thus: V |I|| (See Ex. 122, measure 10.)

The semicadence is, roughly speaking, any interruption that is not a perfect cadence; but it consists most commonly of the *dominant* chord, accented, preceded by any convenient chord (Ex. 122, measure 4).

The disguised cadence is a rather elusive conception, though eminently useful and effective, which may be defined nearly enough as any sort of a joint or interpunction that in some way intentionally evades the *expected* cadential impression. It is therefore, in reality, not a cadence at all, in the structural sense, but a "cadential gesture" which supplants (in a multitude of possible ways, and often very ingeniously) the effect of an interruption that is due and expected at that point (Ex. 122, measure 8). Thus, in Schumann, Op. 68, No. 28:

Two things are here clearly evident to the most superficial observer: (1) a palapable interruption of the melodic strain in the fourth measure; and (2) a complete and decisive termination of the whole melody in the last (10) measure. The first one is a genuine, conventional semicadence (only "semi" because it is not final), upon the dominant chord of the prevailing key (A major). The other one is a perfect cadence, made upon the strongest form of the tonic chord (here E major), with the keynote E at top and bottom, accented, and preceded by the dominant-seventh chord. In each case the melody pauses upon a longer note.

Then there is an *intimated* pause in the eighth measure, also on a longer melody-note, and in the expected place; but there is no check in the rhythmic movement, and consequently no *real* cadence. This is one of the "disguised" forms of the cadence. There is evidence of a desire to rest at this point, but it is completely frustrated by the character of the rhythm and the harmony.

One looks for a cadence in each *fourth* measure, because that number of measures almost always constitutes the limits of a phrase—the smallest complete melodic segment. That is why we expected a cadence in the 8th measure (Ex. 122).

But if it falls in the fifth, sixth, or even seventh measure, you need not be worried. That only means an Irregular Phrase, or, perhaps, some form of Extension. In Ex. 124, A, the second phrase has seven measures.

A complete, firm, perfect cadence marks the end of the Part, as a rule; Ex. 122 is the *first Part* of this composition of Schumann's. The length of a part is optional, and depends naturally, and chiefly, upon the dimensions of the entire piece. Part One may therefore contain any number of phrases, from one (very rarely) up to four, five or six (seldom more); but it consists most commonly of two connected phrases which form the so-called *period* (as in Ex. 122). When a piece of music begins with a single, completely finished phrase, it is most likely that this phrase is an introduction, or prelude—see the fourth "Song without Words" of Mendelssohn; and it so chances that this very same song also illustrates the rare case of a first Part consisting of *one* phrase only, though it assumes the appearance and effect of legitimate length by a slightly altered repetition.

Now, this "first part" *may* be the whole story; but such brevity of design is exceedingly uncommon—excepting in some of our short church hymns and folk-songs; a *second part* is quite certain to follow, and to this is then added, in the great majority of compositions, a *third part*. The contents of the second part are optional; but the *third* part is expected to be, and nearly always is, a *recurrence of the chief contents of the first part*. Do not call Part Three a "repetition" of the First Part; it is a "recurrence." A repetition is an *immediate* restatement. Examine this entire piece (Ex. 122), No. 28 in Schumann's "Jugend Album," and you will recognize it as an example of the typical three-part form. And nothing could be more instructive and convincing than to analyze all of the forty-three numbers of this beautiful work.

Analysis of the Details: The Keys

The technical details of music are three-fold: they embrace the key, the chords, and the neighboring (or embellishing) tones. The first item to establish is the *key;* and this is not an altogether easy task. The only assurance the analyst can depend upon is thorough familiarity with every scale in music; this must precede all analysis. For illustration, in Ex. 122, which begins in A major, there is a change to D major (through the g♮) in the third measure, followed at once by a return to A; and the d♯ in measure 5 leads the harmony into E major, which persists through the sixth measure; in measure 7 there is a very brief assumption of B major (through the a♯), recalled to E on the last beat (with a♮), and followed, through all of measure 8, by c♯ minor (with b♯); this gives way to another brief B major, just as before, in measure 9, followed by the definite final E major.

The duration of a key is entirely optional; it may be limited to one single chord (or beat), or it may extend unchanged through an entire Part. If the chord with a new accidental is followed by the tonic, or some other chord that positively confirms the key which this accidental seems to indicate, then a *complete* modulation is recorded; but if the very next chord pertains to a different key, it is, possibly, only a short *passing* modulation (that is the case with the B major in measures 7 and 9 of Ex. 122; the key lasts only one beat—scarcely long enough to produce the effect of an actual change of key. Hence the term "passing" or "transient" modulation). Finally, any chord with new accidentals, which falls back immediately into the prevailing key, is only an *altered chord*—not a change of key:

"A" is from Schumann's "Scenes of Childhood, Op. 15, No. 8."
It begins in F major; the eb at the end of the first measure changes
the key to Bb—through the essential two chords, V and I, of that
key; the e♮ in the next measure reinstates F; the last chord in the
second measure, with b♮, is *not* in C major, because, instead of
resolving into that key, it passes back *at once* into the tonic chord
of the prevailing key (F). Therefore it is an altered chord in F,
with raised fourth step (b♮). "B" (Ex. 123) is from the
same work, No. 13. Like the case just shown, the c♯ in the third
measure does not change the key, since the tonic chord of G follows; it is an altered chord, with raised fourth step, in G. But in
measure 5, the g♯ and f♮ carry the harmony over into A minor—
a complete modulation. Example C is from Schumann's "Night
Pieces," Op. 23, No. 2; it exhibits a series of quick key-changes,
all of which are properly confirmed by the tonic chord following
each distinctive accidental, as clearly pointed out.

Now practice the quest of keys and key-changes, in this
manner, through a number of the pieces by Schumann, Op. 68
and Op. 15; also the "Songs without Words," and any composition of Mozart, Beethoven or Schubert, until you have acquired
some facility in recognizing the *keys*.

The Chords

As to the chords; it is imperative to recall that there can be
but *three* different chords (or chord-families) anywhere in music
—the tonic, the dominant, and the second- (or sub-) dominant.
And it is equally important to note that it is quite sufficient for
the purpose of general analysis to mark simply these chord-
groups, irrespective of the shape (or inversion) of the separate
bodies; it is just as well to make use of the abbreviations, T., D.,

and SD., instead of the usual Roman numerals. But bear in mind the contents of each class: the tonic consists of the I and the VI; the dominant includes the V in all its shapes, and the III; the second-dominant embraces the II and the IV, in all their forms. These cover the ground completely.

As a clue to the emotional or "spiritual" indices of a composition, it must be recognized that the tonic class is serene, dignified, divine; the dominant, yielding, graceful; the second-dominant, more assertive, bold. In other words, the dominant chords suggest *feminine* qualities; those of the second-dominant *masculine* traits; while the tonic is sexless. It is no extravagant, visionary conception to interpret the three basic chord-families in this way; it is *fact*, not poetic *fancy*. On the contrary, to attribute *colors* to any chords or to any factors of musical perception is absurd. It has never even been proven (nor can it ever be) that the various keys have individual qualities. They differ from each other only in *pitch*, or register. However, the major and minor *modes* surely do suggest respectively light and shade, joy and sadness.

In the following example, the suggested abbreviations, T., D., and SD., are used:

"A" is from the first *Prelude* in Bach's "Well-Tempered Clavichord." The chords are all broken in the same manner as is
shown in the first measure. The analysis is easy, since there are
no inharmonic tones. The chord in the fifth measure is already in
G major; the key changes, as so frequently occurs, at the cadence.
"B" is from Beethoven's "Sonata, Op. 27, No. 2."

Embellishing Tones

Thirdly, account must be rendered of the inharmonic (embellishing) tones, which are foreign to the chords—the neighboring and passing notes. This is a simple process, *after the chords
themselves have been identified.* Of course, these "false" notes
distort the legitimate chord-shape, and it is not always easy to
determine which tone is guilty, and to separate the chaff from
the wheat. The one essential rule is to *look ahead*—see what
happens; for the inharmonic tone should be "resolved," and, in
the majority of cases, it moves *stepwise,* though it does sometimes
fly off, unexpectedly, depending upon the ensuing beats to absorb
it. The only exceptional inharmonic tone is the organ-point, a
sustained tone, usually in the bass-voice. This despotic, but extremely effective inharmonic tone vindicates itself by its obstinacy.
See Ex. 125, C.; the pulsing e♭ in the bass, against the dominant-
seventh chord, is an organ-point.

The "false" notes will generally move into the proper place
in the chord; therefore, observe which tone gives way. For instance, in our Ex. 122, the *a* in the melody in measure 2 is not in
the chord; it should be g♯, and the *a* yields its false position and
moves into the tone g♯, of which it is the upper neighbor. Passing-notes are quickly discernible because they form a scale-line.
And the simple ornamental neighbor betrays its identity by the
manner in which it rolls around, or slips into, its chord tone. For
illustration (all inharmonic tones are marked o):

Ex.125
A Allegro
F Tonic

"A," "B," and "C" are from Beethoven sonatas. "D" is from the *Spinning Song* of Mendelssohn; the c in the bass is an organ-point. "E" is from Wagner's "Die Meistersinger"; the c♯ (properly c♮) is a passing note. "F" is from a waltz of Chopin's.

Important: There are many cases in which more than one logical analytic deduction is possible, partly because so few chords are limited to one single specific meaning, and also in view of the *tempo,* which influences the tone-perspective; a very short key, tone, or chord is more likely to impress the mind as a *passing* unit than as a full, valid member of the tone-body. In doubtful cases you may assume, confidently, that either definition is sufficiently accurate.

Different Types of Music

In the music of Haydn, Mozart, Beethoven, Schubert or Mendelssohn, very few difficulties will be encountered; their analysis is easy, because these classic masters shun irregularities of the confusing sort; their music reflects, in every detail, the authority and dignity of those natural laws which control and determine the association of tones. And the same is true, to a large extent, of the music of Schumann, Brahms, and even of Wagner, although these romantic-classic masters, as I have said, interpret the natural laws of tone-union more broadly and liberally than the older masters do. The music of Chopin is almost in a class by itself, chronologically considered; it is exceedingly subtle and intricate, and the beginner would do well to defer the analysis of Chopin until he has mastered the classics. I would not imply that Chopin's music is faulty—far from it; it follows the "rules" most loyally, with truly amazing flexibility, sound judgment, and an unique sense of tonal beauty and harmoniousness. But the still later romanticists, Franck, Grieg, Debussy, and the moderns, stretch the fundamental laws sadly, often obviously to the breaking point. This is no disparaging criticism of them. They stand for progress. But the novice in analysis will find his task with them difficult, probably hopeless; he should leave their music alone, until he has acquired a great deal of experience and insight.

Finally: when you encounter (as you will, even in simple classic music) a beat that baffles you, let it go—pass it by, for the time being; define the essential units only. Later on, as your judgment quickens, you may return and try again. Bear in mind that *chromatic* progressions are largely responsible for perplexing tone-associations.

SELF-TEST QUESTIONS

1. Define the distinction between harmful and helpful methods of analysis.
2. With what factor should our analysis begin?
3. Define the three varieties of cadence?
4. In which measure do we expect to find a cadence?
5. Why should Part Three *not* be called a "repetition" of Part One?
6. Upon what must we depend for the fixing of the keys?
7. What is the proof of an "altered chord"?

8. Name the three chord-families, and define their respective spiritual qualities.
9. How do we identify inharmonic tones?
10. Which types of music are easy to analyze; which are difficult; and why?
11. What is advisable when we encounter a baffling beat?

A LIST OF MODERN THEORETICAL WORKS
(For General Reference Purposes)

Alchin, C. A.—Applied Harmony. (2 books), each $2.00.
Alchin, C. A.—Keyboard Harmony. (3 books), each $.50.
Ancis, S.—Scheme Modulations. $1.50.
Andersen, Arthur Olaf.—Counterpoint, Strict and Free. $1.00.
Andersen, Arthur Olaf.—First Lessons in Harmony. (2 books), each $1.25.
Andersen, Arthur Olaf.—Short Lessons in Theory. (2 books), each $.75.
Anger, J. Humfrey.—A Treatise on Harmony. (3 books), each $1.50.
Anger, J. Humfrey.—Form in Music. $1.35.
Arensky, A.—Kurzer Leitfaden zum Praktischen Erlernen der Harmonie. $1.25.
Ayres, E. E.—Counterpoint and Canon. $1.25.
Baldwin-Witte.—Harmony Simplified. (2 books), each $.50.
Banister, H. C.—Art of Modulation. $1.25.
Barth, Emil.—Elements of Harmony. $.40.
Bartholomew, Robt.—Elementary Theory and Harmony. $.75.
Bertenshaw, T. H.—Harmony and Counterpoint. $1.35.
Bertenshaw, T. H.—Rhythm, Analysis and Musical Form. $1.20.
Boise, O. B.—Harmony Made Practical. $1.50.
Bradley, Kenneth M.—Harmony and Analysis. $2.00.
Bremer, John W.—Elements of Musical Theory. $.75.
Bernstein, Martin.—Score Reading. $2.50.
Bridge, Dr. J. F.—Double Counterpoint and Canon. $1.50.
Bridge, Dr. J. F.—Strict Counterpoint. $1.00.
Bridge-Sawyer.—Course in Harmony. $2.75.
Broekhoven, J. A.—A System of Harmony for Teacher and Pupil. $1.00.
Brown, Cecil.—Theory of Music. $.50.
Buck, Percy C.—Unfigured Harmony. $2.50.
Bussler-Cornell.—Musical Form. $2.00.
Bussler, Ludwig.—Elementary Harmony. $1.25.
Cator, Thos. Vincent.—The Aura—Modal Scale. $1.00.
Chadwick, G. W.—Harmony. $2.50.
Chaffin, Lucien G.—Song-writing and Song-making. $2.00.
Cherubini, L.—A Treatise on Counterpoint and Fugue. $5.00.
Clappe, Arthur A.—The Principles of Wind Band Transcription. $2.50.
Clarke, H. A.—Counterpoint, Strict and Free. $1.25.
Clarke, H. A.—Harmony. $1.25.
Clarke, H. A.—Theory Explained to Piano Students. $.50.
Coon, Oscar.—Harmony and Instrumentation. (For Orchestra and Military Band) $3.50.
Corder, Frederick.—Modern Musical Composition. $3.00.
Cutter, Benj.—Exercises in Harmony. $1.50.
Cutter, Benj.—Harmonic Analysis. $1.50.
Dana, W. H.—Essentials of Musical Knowledge. $.60.
Daymond, Emily R.—Score Reading Exercises. $1.25.
Diller, Angela.—First Theory Book. $2.00.
Duncan, E.—Melodies and How to Harmonize Them. $1.25.
Dunstan, Ralph.—Basses and Melodies. $2.00.
Dunstan, Ralph.—First Steps in Harmony. $.75.
Dunstan, Ralph.—The A B C of Musical Theory. $.90.
Elson, Louis C.—The Theory of Music. $1.75.
Emery, Stephen A.—Elements of Harmony. $1.25.

Foote, Arthur.—Modulation. $1.25.
Foote & Spaulding.—Modern Harmony. $1.50.
Fowles, Ernest.—Harmony in Pianoforte Study. $1.50.
Gardner, Carl E.—Music Composition. $1.25.
Gardner, Carl E.—The Essentials of Music Theory. $1.00.
Gest, Elizabeth.—Keyboard Harmony for Beginners. $.75.
Giffe, W. T.—Harmony and Composition. $1.25.
Glyn, Margaret H.—The Evolution of Musical Form. $5.00.
Goodrich, A. J.—Musical Analysis. $2.00.
Gow, George Coleman.—The Structure of Music. $1.25.
Grimm, C. W.—Modern Harmony. $1.50.
Hadow.—Sonata Form. $2.00.
Hamilton, Clarence G.—Music Theory for Piano Students. (2 books), each $.50.
Harding, H. A.—Analysis of Form. $1.50.
Heacox, Arthur E.—Harmony for Ear, Eye & Keyboard. $1.50.
Heacox, Arthur E.—Project Lessons in Orchestration. $1.50.
Heacox & Lehmann.—Lessons in Harmony. $2.25.
Herbert, Dr. J. B.—Harmony and Composition. $1.25.
Higgs, James—Modulation. $1.50.
Higgs, James.—Fugue. $1.50.
Hill, Alfred.—Harmony and Melody. $1.50.
Hofheimer, Grace.—Musical Theory at a Glance. $.30.
Holmberg-Giard.—Elementary Theory of Music. $1.50.
How to Play Chords.—A Guide to Extempore Accompaniment. $.60.
Howard, Geo. H.—Course of Harmony. $2.00.
Hull, A. Eaglefield.—Modern Harmony. $4.50.
Iliffe, F.—Analysis of Bach's 48 Preludes and Fugues. $2.25.
Jadassohn, S.—A Manual of Harmony. $2.50.
Jadassohn, S.—A Manual of Single, Double, Triple and Quadruple Counterpoint. $1.75.
Jadassohn, S.—Canon and Fugue. $2.50.
Johnson, A. N.—New Method for Thorough Bass. $1.25.
Kitson, C. H.—Applied Strict Counterpoint. $1.75.
Kitson, C. H.—Contrapuntal Harmony for Beginners. $1.50.
Kitson, C. H.—Counterpoint for Beginners. $1.50.
Kitson, C. H.—Elementary Harmony. $3.25.
Kitson, C. H.—Evolution of Harmony. $4.20.
Kitson, C. H.—Studies in Fugue. $1.75.
Kitson, C. H.—The Art of Counterpoint. $3.35.
Kitson, C. H.—The Elements of Fugal Construction. $2.50.
Kling, H.—Modern Orchestration and Instrumentation. $5.00.
Kling, H.—Transposition. $1.00.
Laurendeau, L. P.—The Practical Band Arranger. $1.25.
Lehman, F. J.—Harmonic Analysis. $1.50.
Lehman, F. J.—A Treatise of Simple Counterpoint. $1.25.
Lehman, F. J.—Analysis of Form in Music. $1.25.
Leighton, Geo. A.—Harmony, Analytical and Applied. $2.50.
Lenormand, Rene.—A Study of Modern Harmony. $2.25.
Loewengard, Max.—Harmony Modernized. $1.50.
Logier, J. B.—Comprehensive Course in Music, Harmony and Practical Composition. $3.50.
Longy-Miquelle.—Principles of Musical Theory. $2.00.
Ludden, W.—Thorough Bass. $1.00.
Macfarren, G. A.—Counterpoint. $3.40.
Macpherson, Stewart.—Form in Music. $2.75.
Macpherson, Stewart.—Melody and Harmony. $4.75.
Macpherson, Stewart.—Practical Counterpoint. $2.25.
Macpherson, Stewart.—Practical Harmony. $2.00.
Macpherson, Stewart.—Studies in Phrasing and Form. $1.75.
Mansfield, Orlando A.—Student's Harmony. $1.75.

Marchant, A. W.—Fugue Subjects. $2.25.
Maryott, Harold B.—Musical Essentials. $1.00.
Maryott, Harold B.—The Essentials of Harmony. $1.50.
Mathews, B. Dingley.—Harmonic Ear Training and Theory. $2.50.
Mayer, Fred C.—Studies in Fugue Writing. $2.50.
McConathy-Embs-Howes-Fouser.—An Approach to Harmony. $1.75.
McCoy, William J.—Cumulative Harmony. $2.40.
McEwen, John B.—Musical Composition. $1.50.
Mendelssohn, Ph. D.—A Complete Method of Musical Composition. (Accord-
    ing to the system of A. B. Marx) $2.00.
Miller, Horace Alden.—New Harmonic Devices. $2.00.
Mokrejs, John.—Lessons in Harmony. $1.75.
Morris, R. O.—Contrapuntal Technic. $2.85.
Morris, R. O.—Foundations of Practical Harmony and Counterpoint. $3.00.
Norris, Homer A.—The Art of Counterpoint. $1.50.
Norris, Homer A.—Practical Harmony. Part 1, Consonance. $1.25.
Norris, Homer A.—Practical Harmony. Part 2, Dissonance. $1.25.
Orem, Dr. Preston Ware.—Harmony Book for Beginners. $1.25.
Orem, Dr. Preston Ware.—Manual of Modulation. $.40.
Orem, Dr. Preston Ware.—Theory and Composition of Music. $1.25.
Palmer, H. R.—Theory of Music. $1.00.
Parkhurst, H. E.—A Complete System of Harmony. $2.00.
Patterson, Frank.—How to Write a Good Tune. $1.50.
Patterson, Frank.—The Perfect Modernist. Harmony Without Rules. $1.00.
Patterson, Frank.—Practical Instrumentation for School, Popular and Sym-
    phony Orchestra. $1.00.
Pauer, E.—Musical Forms. $1.00.
Pearce, Chas. W.—Composers' Counterpoint. $1.50.
Pearce, Chas. W.—Modern Academic Counterpoint. $3.95.
Pearce, Chas. W.—Students' Counterpoint. $1.50.
Peterson, Franklin.—Introduction to the Study of Theory. $1.25.
Peterson, Franklin.—Handbook of Musical Form. $1.00.
Peterson, Franklin.—Catechism of Music. $1.50.
Peterson, Franklin.—Elements of Music, $.75.
Prout, Ebenezer.—Applied Forms. $3.75.
Prout, Ebenezer.—Counterpoint, Strict and Free. $3.75.
Prout, Ebenezer.—Double Counterpoint and Canon. $3.75.
Prout, Ebenezer.—Fugue. $3.75.
Prout, Ebenezer.—Fugal Analysis. $3.75.
Prout, Ebenezer.—Harmony, Its Theory and Practice. $3.00.
Prout, Ebenezer.—Musical Form. $3.75.
Prout, Ebenezer.—A Treatise on Instrumentation. $1.00.
Piston, Walter.—Principles of Harmonic Analysis. $2.00.
Reed, Clare Osborne.—Constructive Harmony and Improvisation. $1.50.
Richardson, A. Madeley.—Helps to Fugue Writing. (Based on Bach's W. T.
    C.) $1.50.
Richter, Ernst F.—Canon and Fugue. $2.00.
Richter, Ernst F.—Manual of Harmony. $2.00.
Richter, Ernst F.—Manual of Simple and Double Counterpoint. $2.00.
Riemann, Dr. H.—Analysis of Bach's W. T. C. (2 books), each $1.50.
Riemann, Dr. H.—Harmony Simplified. $3.00.
Riemann, Dr. H.—Simple and Double Counterpoint. $2.00.
Rimsky-Korsakow, N.—Practical Manual of Harmony. $2.50.
Ritter, Dr. F. L.—Practical Harmony. $1.00.
Robinson, Franklin W.—Aural Harmony. (2 parts), each $3.00.
Robyn, Louise.—Master Key to Harmony and Ear Training. $1.00.
Rockstro, W. S.—Practical Harmony. $1.50.
Rockstro, W. S.—Rules of Counterpoint. $1.50.
Scholes, Percy A.—The Beginner's Guide to Harmony. $.85.
Schönberg, Arnold.—Harmonielehre. $6.00. (German Text Only.)

Schuler, Geo. S.—Four Part Harmony and Composition. $1.75.
Shefte, Art.—Keyboard Harmony Simplified. $1.00.
Shepard, F. H.—Children's Harmony. $.75.
Shepard, F. H.—Graded Lessons in Harmony. $1.25.
Shepard, F. H.—Harmony Simplified. $1.50.
Shinn, Frederick G.—A Method of Teaching Harmony—Part 1. Diatonic.
     $3.00.
Shinn, Frederick G.—A Method of Teaching Harmony—Part 2. Chromatic.
     $3.75.
Skinner, O. R.—The First Year in Theory. $1.00.
Smith, Ralph Fisher.—Elementary Music Theory. $1.50.
Smith, Uselma Clarke.—Keyboard Harmony. $1.25.
Spaulding, Walter R.—Tonal Counterpoint. $2.50.
Spencer, S. Reid.—Harmony. $.75.
Stainer, John.—Guide to Beginners in Composition. $1.00.
Stainer, John.—Harmony. (Cloth) $1.50; (Paper) $.50.
Stanford, Charles V.—Musical Composition. $1.50.
Strube, Gustav.—The Theory and the Use of Chords. $1.75.
Tapper, Thomas.—First Year Analysis (Musical Form). $1.00.
Tapper, Thomas.—First Year Counterpoint. $1.00.
Tapper, Thomas.—First Year Harmony. $1.25.
Tapper, Thomas.—First Year Melody Writing. $1.00.
Tapper, Thomas.—First Year Musical Theory. $1.00.
Tapper, Thomas.—Second Year Harmony. $1.00.
Thompson, John Winter.—A Course in Harmony. $1.25.
Tschaikowsky, P.—Guide to the Practical Study of Harmony. $1.50.
Tweedy, Donald.—Manual of Harmonic Technic. (Based on the Practice of
     J. S. Bach) $3.00.
Vernham, J. E.—First Steps in the Harmonization of Melodies. $.75.
Vogler, Julius.—Modern Method of Modulation. $.50.
Watt, H. F.—The Foundations of Music. $8.40.
Weber, H.—A Text Book for the Study of Harmony. $1.50.
Wedge, George A.—Applied Harmony. (2 books), each $2.00.
Wedge, George A.—Ear-training and Sight-singing applied to elementary musi-
     cal theory. $2.50.
Wedge, George A.—Advanced Ear-training and Sight-singing. $2.50.
Wedge, George A.—Keyboard Harmony. $2.50.
Wedge, George A.—Rhythm in Music. $1.50.
Weidig, Adolf.—Harmonic Material and Its Uses. $3.00.
White & Jones.—Harmonic Dictation. $1.60.
White, Wm. C.—Military Band Arranging. $2.00.
Wohlfahrt, H.—Guide to Musical Composition, $1.25.
York, Francis L.—Counterpoint Simplified. $1.50.
York, Francis L.—Harmony Simplified. $1.50.
Zeiner, Ed. J. A.—The Elements of Musical Theory. $.32.

Any of the foregoing books may be secured from the publisher of this book.
Prices may vary with conditions and International Exchange.